MAKING
DOLL'S HOUSE
MINIATURES
WITH POLYMER CLAY

MAKING
DOLL'S HOUSE
MINIATURES
WITH POLYMER CLAY

SUE HEASER

To John, Kathy and Tamsin
for their encouragement and forbearance!

First published in the UK 1997
Cassell Illustrated
Octopus Publishing Group
2-4 Heron Quays
London E14 4JP

This paperback edition published 2000

Reprinted 2002

Distributed in the United States
by Sterling Publishing Co., Inc.
387 Park Avenue South, New York, NY 10016–8810

A British Library Cataloguing in Publication Data block for this book
may be obtained from the British Library

ISBN 0-304-35570-4

Printed by Toppan Printing Co., (H.K.) Ltd.
Designed by Isobel Gillan
Photography by Jeremy Thomas

Acknowledgements

I would like to thank the following people for their help with making
and furnishing the room boxes used in the photographs:

CATHARINE MacKENZIE
9957 Sullivan Street
Burnaby
British Columbia
Canada V3J 1J1

Designs and makes miniature furniture. Kitchen table (page 30);
living room sofa, fireplace, desk and parquet floor (pages 48-49);
sideboard and parquet floor (pages 62-63); the conservatory (pages 76-77);
bed, bedside table, dressing table and wooden floor (pages 90-91).

CHRIS-A-LIZ
85–86 New Road
Kidderminster
Worcestershire DY10 1AE
UK

Large doll's house and miniatures shop; also mail order.
Dining room table and chairs (pages 62-63).

CAROLYN POSTGATE
5 Whitwell Way
Coton
Cambridge CB3 7PW
UK

Designs and supplies kits for making authentic miniature
oriental carpets. Miniature carpets (pages 48-49 and 90-91).

The room boxes were constructed by

DEREK TUDOR
Tudor Rose Miniatures
Unit 5 Taverham Craft Centre
Fir Covert Road
Norwich NR8 6HT
UK

TONY BREWSTER
Tarka
Otter Close
Salhouse
Norfolk N13 6SF
UK

The room boxes were decorated by the author.

CONTENTS

INTRODUCTION

Polymer clays were originally developed in the 1930s, but it is only relatively recently that they have become widely available to the home miniaturist. Often called modelling clay, they are sold under such brand names as Fimo, Sculpey, Cernit and Formello, and they have revolutionized home crafting for the doll's house.

The clays, which are available in an extraordinary range of colours, are hardened permanently by simply baking at a low temperature in a home oven. Once hardened, they can be cut, sanded, painted, drilled, added to and re-baked. They are non-toxic and virtually odourless and have a fine texture that is ideal for making miniatures.

Because of the versatility of these clays, it is possible to simulate a wide variety of materials, ranging from metals such as brass and cast iron to food, plants, wood and ceramic. This gives the home miniaturist exciting new opportunities that would formerly have required a whole range of skills. You can be a miniature potter, metalworker or carpenter without changing your medium!

The projects in this book range from food and vegetables, which are suitable for beginners, through to more challenging miniatures. If you have not used these clays before, it is best to attempt the simpler projects first and then to progress to the more advanced pieces as your skill develops.

All crafts require practice in order to advance, but working with polymer clay builds on basic skills such as rolling clay balls and modelling that most of us acquire in childhood. If you are a beginner and your first attempts seem clumsy, persevere and you will find you improve rapidly. You would not expect to knit an elaborate sweater as your first knitting project, so approach this medium in the same way as any worthwhile craft – practice makes perfect.

ABOUT THE PROJECTS

The scale of 1:12 or 25mm (1in) to 30cm (1ft) is used throughout this book and is the most common scale used in doll's houses today. If your doll's house is in a smaller scale, you will need to scale the projects down.

I have chosen the late Victorian and Edwardian period in which to base the setting of the rooms, but many miniatures are timeless, and if your doll's house is of another period, you will find most of the projects are equally useful. Food, crockery, plants and the basic everyday items such as stools, wooden spoons, cutlery and kitchenware will all settle happily into virtually any period with only minor adaptations.

CHAPTER 1

MATERIALS

THE MAIN BRANDS OF POLYMER CLAY

All the projects in this book were made using Fimo, but any of the different brands of polymer clay could be used because they are all basically very similar. However, avoid using the softer clays for more delicate work or if your hands are prone to becoming very warm.

The main attributes of all the brands of polymer modelling clays are as follows:

- They are produced in a wide variety of colours which can be intermixed to produce an even greater range of colours.
- They have a very fine texture, making detailed modelling possible.
- They can be rolled flat into thin sheets and draped like fabric; sliced, grated, extruded, modelled and sculpted; tooled and impressed like metal and leather; and coloured with metallic powders and chalks.
- They are stable while baking; there is negligible shrinkage and virtually no colour change.
- The different brands can be intermixed, although it is prudent to test samples first.
- They remain soft until baked, and they have a shelf-life of several years.
- Once hardened by baking at approximately 130°C/275°F in a domestic oven, they can be cut, sawn, added to, re-baked, glued and painted with water-based paints.
- After hardening they remain slightly flexible and are durable and robust.

Polymer clays are widely available from art and craft shops and mail order suppliers. The availability of different brands varies from one country to another. Further new brands of clay are regularly being developed.

Fimo

Fimo is manufactured by Eberhard Faber of Germany, and its firm texture makes it particularly suitable for the miniaturist as it holds its shape well. Other products include textured stone-effect colours and Mix Quick, which is a softening agent for mixing with the clay.

Formello

Known as Modello in some countries, Formello is manufactured in Germany by Rudolf Reiser. It has a medium texture and bright colours.

Cernit

Cernit is made by T + F GmbH in Germany. It has a soft to medium texture and a semi-translucent quality with a porcelain-like effect. An opaque white is available for mixing with the colours to make them less translucent if required.

Sculpey III

Sculpey III is manufactured by Polyform Products of Illinois, USA. It has a soft texture so it can be difficult to use for more detailed miniatures. The baked clay is rather brittle.

Premo

This is the newest clay from Polyform Products of the USA and is medium textured with an excellent colour range for mixing. It is very good for making miniatures and strong after baking.

Granitex

Also made by Polyform Products, this is a granite-textured clay. It comes in a range of subtle colours and is suitable for stone effect miniatures.

Creall-Therm

Manufactured in Holland by Havo, B.V., Creall-Therm has a medium to firm texture making it excellent for miniatures. The baked clay is strong.

Du-Kit

Manufactured by Creative Products in New Zealand, Du-Kit has a medium texture and comes with a good range of hues for colour mixing.

Modelene

The Australian polymer clay, Modelene is medium textured and extremely strong after baking.

STORING CLAY

Store your clay in a cool, dark place to lengthen its shelf-life and to prevent it going crumbly. Opened packets are best stored in an airtight tin. Avoid plastic containers because they may be damaged by being in contact with polymer clays.

EQUIPMENT

Most of the basic equipment needed for making polymer clay miniatures can be found in your home. Because it is such a robust material, it is also possible to make your own tools and formers from the clay itself, and suggestions for these are given in the instructions.

The following list includes all the basic tools that were used to make the projects in this book. The section on simulating materials with polymer clays gives further details of tools. If specific tools are needed for a project, they are described in the instructions. Basic equipment is not listed every time.

Basic Equipment

- A board to work on. A smooth melamine chopping board is ideal; alternatively, a formica table mat can be used.
- A craft knife with a rounded blade as shown in the photograph. This shape of blade is the most versatile and can be blunted slightly before use by running it over a steel because razor-sharpness is not necessary for most techniques.
- A ruler to check the size of balls, logs and so on.
- A small rolling pin. A smooth-barrelled pencil or pen is best for tiny rollings, while a straight-sided glass or a small bottle can be used for flattening larger pieces.

- Nail varnish remover or baby wipes for cleaning hands and the board.
- Talcum powder for dusting the board and hands to prevent the clay sticking.

Modelling Tools

For miniature modelling you will need a selection of tiny tools. My favourites are:
- Blunt-ended wool or tapestry needles
- Darning needle
- Pins
- Small, rounded paintbrush handles

Baking Equipment

- A baking tray lined with non-stick baking parchment.
- Aluminium foil for supporting work while it is baked.
- Ceramic tiles are useful. If you make delicate miniatures on a ceramic tile, they can be put straight into the oven and baked on the tile.

NOTE Kitchen equipment that is used for working with clay should not be used with food. Although polymer clay is non-toxic, it should never come into contact with items used for food preparation. Keep your clay tools exclusively for that purpose.

MATERIALS

Varnishes

Texture is all important in making miniatures, and the appropriate use of varnish when simulating certain materials will give convincing results. The matt surface of the clay is perfect for many materials,

and varnish should be used only when a high gloss is required. Matt varnish is also available and is useful as a protection for painted polymer clay when a gloss finished is not needed – on doll's faces or painted designs on matt pottery, for example.

Do not use a varnish that is based on oils or white spirit because it will not dry on the baked clay.

The best varnishes to use are those produced by the polymer clay manufacturers since these are made to be compatible with the clays. Both spirit- and water-based varnishes are available. Use methylated spirits to clean brushes after applying spirit-based varnish.

Water-based acrylic hobby varnish is an economical alternative.

Paints

Polymer clay provides an excellent surface for painting, but a few basic rules apply:

- It is essential to de-grease the clay surface first by brushing it with nail varnish remover or methylated spirit.
- Do not use enamel or oil paints because these will not dry on the baked clay.
- The best paints to use are water-based acrylics, either artist's acrylics or hobby paints, which provide the most permanent results. Ordinary water paint can shift and stain in time, even under a coat of varnish.
- For the most permanent results, it is best to varnish the miniatures with matt or gloss varnish before painting and then to apply another coat of varnish to seal the paint.
- Use good quality artist's watercolour brushes in tiny sizes for applying the paint. Synthetic round brushes, sizes 0 to 0000, are best for tiny motifs.

Glass Paints

Special glass paints can be used to great effect to simulate stained glass – see, for example, the Tiffany lamp project on page 60. Again, use only water- or spirit-based paints.

Metallic Paints

Acrylic metallic paints are useful when you want to simulate brass, silver, gilding, copper and so on. They do not give as brilliant an effect as metallic powders but they can be used for delicate painted detail when the powders would be too messy.

Metallic Powder Paint

An effective metallic paint can be made by mixing the metallic powders with varnish, but this is not usually thin enough for detailed designs on, for example, china. It is most useful when the soft miniature is too delicate for powder to be applied before baking.

Powder Colours

Polymer clays have a unique ability to accept powder colour before they are baked. The colour is brushed onto the surface of the clay with a soft brush and then the item is baked as usual. This gives the opportunity to make delicate graded tones on the surface, which can be used to great effect for food, fruit and flowers. The results look far more natural than painting for these miniatures.

Artist's Pastels

These are the best colours to use for coloured powder effects and are easily found in art supply shops in a wonderful range of colours. Be sure to buy soft artist's pastels and not oil pastels. Rub the pastel on some scrap paper to release the powder and then use a soft brush to apply it to the unbaked clay. You will find that you can grade the colour from a light dusting to quite dark tones by applying thicker amounts to the areas you want to be dark. Suggestions for specific colours to use are given in the projects.

Metallic Powders

Metallic powders give some excellent effects with modelling clay. Both Fimo and Cernit produce a range of metallic powder colours, and although they are quite expensive, a little goes a long way and the results are far superior to metallic paint. Other metallic powders are available from hobby shops.

The powder is brushed onto the unbaked clay surface with a soft artist's paintbrush. The powdered clay must be varnished after baking. See page 28 for suggestions on how to simulate metal with metallic powders.

MISCELLANEOUS MATERIALS

There are many other useful materials that you can combine with polymer clay miniatures to make them look more authentic, and suggestions are given in the projects. Always be on the look out for materials that might be useful for they can turn up in the most unexpected places: egg-crafting catalogues are a useful source of miniature raw materials, as are bead shops, haberdashery stores, hardware shops and cake decorating shops.

Be aware of natural substances as well – my favourite texturing tool came from the sea shore and is a pebble covered with barnacles!

Over the page is a list of useful materials that were used to make the projects and where to find them.

- Paper pictures for miniature frames can be found in catalogues and magazines. Doll's house shops and suppliers sometimes sell small pictures to scale.
- Jewellery findings, beads and charms. The fine chains, beading wire, tiny rings (jump rings), peg and loop fastenings and S-fittings that are so useful in some projects are all obtainable from jewellery craft suppliers. Bead shops will have glass and crystal beads, which can be used for tiny bottles, and charms for making stamps.
- Doll's house light bulbs with attached wires and plugs are used for the lamp projects and are obtainable from doll's house and hobby suppliers.
- Paper clock faces can be cut out of magazines and catalogues or bought on a sheet from doll's house and hobby suppliers.
- Florists' wire, which is green, paper-coated wire, is available in cake craft shops or from hobby suppliers. Use the finer gauges – no. 32 grade is best for miniatures. Avoid plastic-coated wire.
- Tiny hinges in a variety of shapes can be found in hobby and doll's house shops.
- Mohair in various colours is available from doll and doll's house suppliers.
- Trimmings, such as very narrow ribbons, tiny picot edgings, braids, fringe and soutache, can be obtained from doll's house suppliers or specialist doll's house haberdashers.

Most suppliers of these items advertise in hobby or doll's house magazines and offer a mail order service.

GLUES

Baked polymer clay can be glued easily, and the following types of glue are the most useful for miniatures.

Superglue

Use one of proprietary brands of rapid-setting or cyanoacrylate adhesive when you are gluing two pieces of clay together or when you are gluing clay to hard materials like metal. It gives a very strong bond almost instantly, but because it does the same to human flesh, you need to treat these adhesives with some respect. Squeeze a drop onto a piece of foil and use a cocktail stick to apply it to the clay. The drop on the foil remains wet for some time, so this is not wasteful and gives you far more control.

PVA Adhesive

Use a PVA adhesive when you are gluing a soft substance, such as fabric, fibres and trimmings, to baked clay. The bond is not as permanent and the glue takes longer to dry than Superglue, but the adhesive is more controllable and will not stain fabric or paper. My favourite is Aleene's Tacky Glue, which is available from craft shops, but most PVA adhesives will be suitable.

Glue Sticks

These are the white glue sticks that are available from stationers for gluing paper and card. Use the stick to smear onto baked clay to make fresh clay adhere more easily.

CHAPTER 2

TECHNIQUES

BASIC TECHNIQUES

It is important to read these instructions before attempting the designs in this book since, to avoid constant repetition, the individual instructions for each design assume that you understand these basic techniques.

General Hints

◆ Always clean your hands thoroughly before working with clay because the smallest trace of dirt will be transferred onto the clay and stain it. Wiping over with cleansing wipes or nail varnish remover should solve the problem. Remember to cleanse again between colours.

◆ Try to avoid poking and patting the object you are making. Once a piece of clay has been added, do not try to reshape it because the result will be messy. If you are not happy with it, remove the piece and start again.

◆ It is not necessary to squash pieces together to effect a join. The pieces will weld together when they are baked. Gentle but firm pressure is all that is needed.

◆ Use the natural tackiness of the clay as an aid. A piece pressed lightly onto the board will stay in place while you work on it.

◆ Do not attempt to cook or soften clay in the microwave.

Softening the Clay

Before use, always work each piece of clay in your hands to soften it. This is best achieved by repeatedly rolling and folding the clay. The amount of kneading required before the clay becomes soft and pliable varies between brands and between colours within brands. Insufficient kneading will result in bubbles and irregularities on the baked surface.

If you need a large piece, cut small chunks off the block and work them individually before combining them. In cold weather, you can warm the clay gently on a hot water bottle to make it more pliable. If the clay is crumbly, you have not worked it enough.

Sometimes the clay seems to remain crumbly, despite thorough kneading, and this usually means that it is old stock. Try mixing it with Mix Quick, the mixing agent made by Fimo, or kneading in a little baby oil or vegetable oil. If it is still hard and lumpy, take it back to the shop, as it is either old stock or has been stored in conditions that are too hot. Make sure you don't leave any of your clay in the full glare of the sun!

Clay that becomes too soft in your hands to hold its shape can be rested in the refrigerator for a while to cool it. Alternatively, leave it sitting on a piece of paper for a few days to soak up the excess plasticizer. A dusting of talcum powder over the clay helps to prevent it from sticking.

Making Balls

The clay ball is the starting point for many designs. Squeeze the clay into a rough ball shape and then rotate it between your palms, applying heavier pressure first, and then lighter pressure as the ball takes shape.

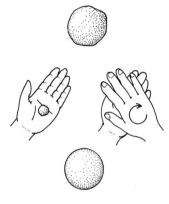

Many of the projects start with a clay ball of a particular size and the measurement given is always the diameter. Using your ruler for guidance, shape a ball roughly the right size and pinch off or add clay as necessary.

Making Cylinders or 'Logs'

Making cylindrical shapes is an important part of working with clay. Practise rolling the clay into even logs of different thicknesses. Start with a ball of clay and roll it between your hands. Place the resulting oval shape on your working surface and

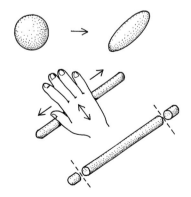

roll it smoothly, always keeping your hand moving back and forth along the length of the log and not pressing too hard.

Most project instructions give the thickness and lengths of logs required. A simple way to measure thickness is to cut rectangular notches of several different widths in the edge of a piece of card and to place the required width over the log. Use your ruler to measure the lengths required.

Rolling Sheets

Some projects require flat sheets of clay. Form a thick log of clay and press it down onto the board. Roll out the clay with your 'rolling pin' as though it were pastry. Larger pieces will need a bottle or jam jar as a rolling pin, but small pieces are best rolled with a smooth pencil or pen barrel. Have some talcum powder handy for dusting the clay surface to prevent sticking. If bubbles appear in the surface, prick them with a pin and continue rolling.

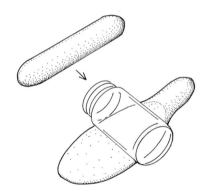

Try to roll out the clay to the same thickness right across the sheet. A useful aid is to place thin strips of wood of the required thickness on either side of the clay. This prevents you from rolling the clay too thin. Wood strips are available from doll's house and hobby shops.

Several projects require you to roll out clay on a ceramic tile and cut out shapes using templates.

Rolling the clay directly onto the tile avoids having to move the cut-out shapes before baking and prevents distortion. Remove the waste clay from around the shapes, and use the side of the knife blade to push back into place any edges that distort slightly.

When you are cutting out curved shapes, try to keep the knife as vertical as possible. Long, straight cuts are best achieved using a long-bladed knife and cutting straight down.

Working with the Knife

The craft knife with a curved blade is an invaluable tool. It is not only useful for cutting the clay to the required sizes but is also useful as a delicate applying tool when your hands would soon distort the clay. Tiny slices and delicate strips of clay are best applied by scooping them up on the tip of the knife. They should cling to the blade sufficiently for you to turn over the knife to position them, and then you can use the blade to press them lightly down.

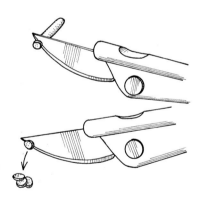

Stamping

Using stamps to impress patterns and motifs on the clay is a delightful technique, which will help you imitate many forms of craft work, such as embossed and engraved silver and carved wood. Always dust the clay surface lightly with talcum powder before stamping to prevent sticking.

There are various ways of making stamps to use with polymer clay miniatures and the main types used in this book are given here.

Simple Leaf Stamp

Form a log of scrap clay, about 5mm (³⁄₁₆in) thick, and cut off one end. Shape this into a leaf-shape and mark veins with the point of a wool needle. Bake for 10 minutes.

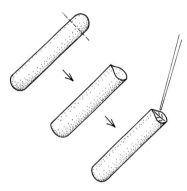

Carved Maple Leaf Stamp

Form a 6mm (¼in) thick log of scrap clay, about 40mm (1½in) long, and bake for 10 minutes. Cut the end off the log to give a neat end and cut a maple leaf shape in the end by slicing away the outside edge. Cut notches for the veins.

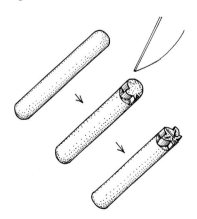

Leather Tooling Stamps

These tiny stamps are used for stamping the leather books on page 56 and give an effect of tooled leather.

Form some thin logs, about 1.5mm (¹⁄₁₆in) thick, and cut some tiny bars from unkneaded clay, square in section. Bake these for 10 minutes and then cut the ends to square them. Cut tiny wedges out of the ends to make crosses and patterns for tooling. A variety of designs is shown in the illustration.

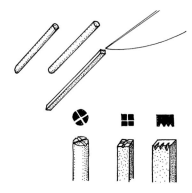

Stamps from Charms

Several of the projects in this book use stamps made from jewellery charms. You will need to use particularly small charms, and these can often be found in bead shops or advertised in egg-decorating catalogues and needlework catalogues. A childhood charm bracelet can often supply a treasure-trove of small charms, and tiny silver stud earrings, which come in many designs, are another useful source. Low-relief charms work best.

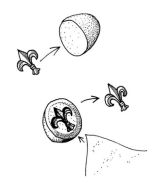

Form a small ball of clay about the same diameter as the charm. Press it onto the board to flatten one side. Press the charm into the flattened clay and then press the clay down onto the board again so that the charm is pushed in smoothly. If you are using an earring, simply make an impression with it in the clay. Bake the stamp for 10 minutes, with the charm in place, and when it is cool, remove the charm and sand round the edges to chamfer them almost up to the image.

Other Sources

There are many other sources of tiny relief images from which to make stamps. Try looking closely at your jewellery for engraving and tiny motifs. Engraved cutlery is another good source.

The Art Nouveau tiles project (see page 112) includes instructions for yet another form of stamp.

SANDING

Polymer clay can be sanded very effectively to smooth out imperfections and obtain a beautiful sheen. The best types of sandpaper to use are the finer grades, 400 and 600. If you use wet and dry sandpaper, the clay can be sanded under a running tap for quicker effects and to avoid clogging the sandpaper.

Once they are sanded, the darker clays will show a lighter surface covered in small scratches. To remove these, rub the clay firmly with a scrap of denim material or a piece of polyester quilt wadding (batting). This will result in a shining patina, and it will give the various marbled wood effects the look of French polishing. It is also possible to polish the surface with a buffing wheel attachment on a small drill. A little furniture polish will finish the surface beautifully and is a pleasing alternative to varnish.

MIXING CLAY COLOURS

Polymer clays come in a wide range of colours, which can be combined to make still further colours, giving an almost unlimited range. You can create a palette of clay in the same way as an artist mixes paint. Making new colours is a simple process: work the different coloured clays together until all streakiness has disappeared. It is often better to make up a small quantity first to judge proportions.

- When you are mixing pastels, add small quantities of coloured clay to white until you have the colour you require; you will need far more white than colour.
- Remember that darker clays are stronger and will dominate, so you will need far less red than yellow, for example, when you are mixing orange.
- Some lovely effects can be obtained by mixing transparent clay with a colour to create a translucent effect rather like porcelain. Cernit clays have this translucent effect in all colours, and the clays are made opaque by adding opaque white.
- It is possible to save money by mixing your own colours instead of buying a large range of different colours. Many mixtures are given below, and more are included in the projects.

The clay used for the projects is Fimo and because all the manufacturers use different names for the colours of their clays, I have used descriptive names for the colours and given the proprietary Fimo names in brackets if they are not the same. If you use a different brand, the colours will not be identical and you will need to adjust quantities.

All the colours used in this book are listed below, but most individual projects require only one or two colours. You will need to buy the colours in the first list to obtain the truest colours, while those in the second list can be purchased or mixed.

Main Colours

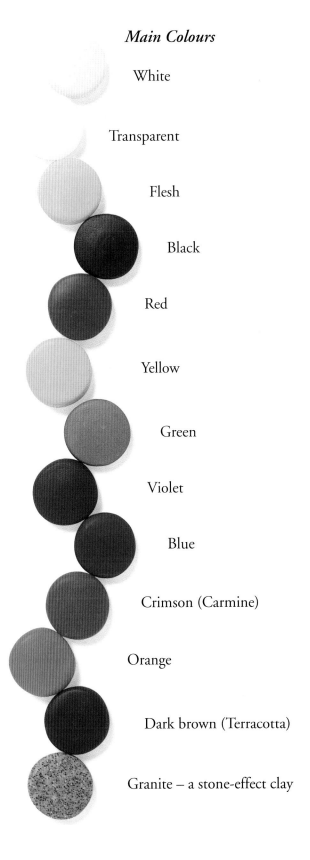

White

Transparent

Flesh

Black

Red

Yellow

Green

Violet

Blue

Crimson (Carmine)

Orange

Dark brown (Terracotta)

Granite – a stone-effect clay

Mixed Colours

Golden-yellow
= 8 yellow + 1 orange

Pink
= 8 white + scant 1 red

Turquoise
= 4 blue + 1 green

Navy blue
= 4 blue + 1 crimson

Leaf green
= 4 green + 1 dark brown

Light brown (Caramel)
= 2 dark brown + 1 white

Ochre
= 1 light brown + 1 yellow

Beige (Champagne)
= 1 ochre + 1 white

The above figures represent how many equal parts of each colour are needed to make a mixture. For example, to mix golden-yellow you will need to combine 8 parts of yellow with one part of orange. To do this, roll a log, 6mm (¼in) thick, each of yellow and of orange. Cut eight equal lengths of yellow and one, the same length, of orange. Mix these together for the golden-yellow colour.

This method is also used in the projects. Where no proportions are given, the colour balance is less critical, and you should mix to your own taste.

Marbling

This is a simple process that involves mixing two or more colours of clay until the clay is liberally streaked. The streaks will become thinner and thinner as you mix the clays until they combine into a new colour, so you must stop mixing before you reach this point. Full instructions for this process are given in the wood grain instructions on page 27.

BAKING

Place the modelled clay onto a baking sheet that has been lined with baking parchment. All the polymer clays listed should be baked in the oven for 10–20 minutes at 130°C/275°F, but check the manufacturer's instructions first. Larger pieces will need longer, as will designs that you wish to be as strong as possible because they have a particularly fragile shape – some of the plants, for example. Clay baked on a ceramic tile will also need more time because the tile will take longer to heat up. The instructions for the projects give suggested baking times.

It is advisable to measure your oven's temperature carefully with a separate oven thermometer to make sure that the temperature is correct. Oven thermostats vary quite widely, and if the clay is baked at too high a temperature, the clay will burn and toxic fumes can be given off; if the temperature is too low, the clay will take a long time to harden or it may remain fragile and applied pieces will drop off easily.

The clay will not harden until it is completely cool, but it can be baked again if you are not satisfied with the hardness. Pale colours may become slightly discoloured after prolonged baking.

Varnish and powders are not affected by the baking temperatures, so varnished and powdered pieces can be re-baked if necessary. Some acrylic paints may discolour if baked, however.

BAKING TEST

This is a useful test for checking your oven temperature when baking polymer clay. Form two small balls of clay and press them together lightly. Preheat your oven to 130°C/275°F and bake them for 20 minutes. When the clay has cooled, try to pull the balls apart.

1. The balls separate easily and there is no sign of the two balls fusing = oven too cool.
2. The balls are difficult to separate and leave tear marks in the clay when they do = oven just right.
3. The balls are very hard to separate and have a shiny or discoloured appearance = oven too hot.

SAFETY

Polymer modelling clays are all made from fine PVC particles suspended in plasticizers, which give the clay its malleability and softness. Baking the clay causes the PVC particles to fuse together into a permanent plastic, which is a stable product, but there may be traces of plasticizer left that can continue to leach out. All the proprietary clays are labelled as being non-toxic but, as with any art and craft medium, it is sensible to follow some basic precautions.

- **Never** allow the clays to overheat. When they burn, they produce toxic fumes. If you accidentally let the clay overheat, turn off the oven at once and ventilate the room thoroughly. Avoid breathing any fumes.
- Always wash your hands after using polymer clays.
- Do not allow polymer clays to come into contact with foodstuffs, even after baking.
- Do not use the same utensils for polymer clays and food.
- Supervise young children when they are handling the clays.

SIMULATING WITH POLYMER CLAYS

The versatility and fine texture of polymer clays means that they can be used to simulate a wide variety of materials.

Ceramics

Plain white clay, painted with a design in acrylic paint and then varnished with gloss varnish, makes excellent white china. Any colour of clay can be used to make coloured china and pottery, but if you want a partial glaze, it is best to make the pottery in a clay body colour and use acrylic paint and then a coat of varnish for the glaze, painting it to look 'dipped' (see the earthenware storage jars on page 39). The following mixtures are for different clay colours:

White china = white
Creamware = 4 white + 1 ochre
Terracotta = 1 red + 2 light brown
Cream stoneware = 1 white + 1 ochre
Grey stoneware = 8 white + 2 ochre + 1 black

For very coarse pottery, try mixing a little sand into the clay for more texture. Coarsely ground spices will give dark speckles but make sure that any material you work into the clay is bone dry. The fine powder in the bottom of packs of tea bags gives very good, tiny speckles for stoneware.

Forming China and Pottery

In order to make miniature vessels and plates with polymer clay, you will need a series of formers, which you can make quite easily out of the clay itself. The following formers are used in the projects in this book.

6mm (¼in) Cup and Saucer Former

Make a 13mm (½in) ball of clay and shape it into 6mm (¼in) thick log, keeping the ends nicely rounded. Place in a cool oven, bring up to temperature and bake for 10 minutes. (This keeps the log as round as possible.) While it is still warm, cut off one end neatly to give a flat, round surface for impressing the centre of saucers. The rounded end is used to shape the cups after potting them (see Potting, below). You can rub the flat end on sandpaper to make it smooth if necessary.

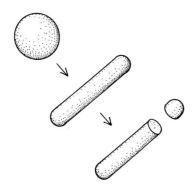

The Plate Formers

Make formers as above in the following thicknesses:

    10mm (⅜in)

    13mm (½in)

Marbles

These are used to shape bowls and can be found in most toy shops. The following sizes (the diameters) are used in the projects:

    13mm (½in)

    20mm (¾in)

    22mm (⅞in)

To keep a marble steady while you are making a bowl, press it onto a small scrap of clay.

Making a Bowl

Form a 13mm (½in) ball of clay and press it flat onto the board until it forms a circle of clay 30mm (1¼in) across, slightly domed in the middle and thinner at the edge. Slice off the board and dust the underside with talcum powder. Mould the circle of clay round a 20mm (¾in) marble into a bowl shape, keeping the rim as straight as possible.

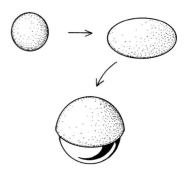

Mark a rim line, if required, with a wool needle and press the base of the bowl onto the board to flatten it. Bake the bowl on the marble for 10 minutes. Prise carefully off the marble and smooth the rim by rubbing the dish, upside down on sandpaper. Rub the sanded surfaces with quilt wadding to polish them.

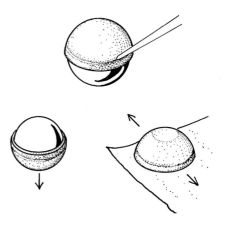

Potting

I have developed a technique of making pots with polymer clay, which is great fun and does not take long to master. As your skill grows, you will find that you can make pots, cups, vases and vessels of many shapes and sizes with remarkably thin sides.

The basic technique described here is used in several of the projects, where suggestions are made for shaping different types of vessel.

To make a simple cup, first form a 6mm (¼in) ball of clay, making it as round as you can. Insert a wool needle into the ball, pushing it only halfway in. Hold the needle firmly, with the ball resting on the board on its side. Move your hand from side to side, pressing downwards slightly so that the ball is made to turn on the end of the needle, rather like a wheel on an axle. This will begin to enlarge the hole and thin the sides. Be careful not to push the needle right through the clay. If the cup begins to be lop-sided, stand it upright and press it back into shape before continuing.

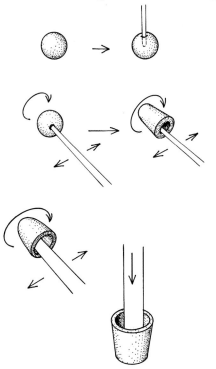

For larger vessels, start with larger ball of clay and, once the hole is 5mm (³⁄₁₆in) across, replace the needle with a paintbrush handle or a thicker needle that has been dusted in talcum powder. Continue the process to make the hole even larger and thin the sides. The bottom of the vessel is flattened by pressing it, still on the former, onto the board.

After baking, the vessel can be sanded to remove irregularities and the rim made level by inverting it onto sandpaper and rubbing.

Painting China and Pottery

First, varnish the pot with either matt or gloss varnish, depending on what the final finish will be. Mark the design with a fine pencil line, which can easily be erased if you make a mistake. Try to get your pencil marks at regular intervals if you are painting a repeating pattern.

Brush the pot lightly with nail varnish remover or methylated spirits. Paint the design using a fine artist's paintbrush, preferably made with synthetic hairs. If you make a mistake or dislike the result, you can scrape the paint off quite easily and start again. Finally, allow to dry overnight and then varnish again.

Food

Food is usually the first type of miniature that people attempt in polymer clay and with good reason, for food is simple and fun to make. The projects include many of the basic types of food, from bread and vegetables to elaborate cakes and desserts, but you will have enormous fun making your own designs. Colour and texture are vital in making convincing miniature food, and the projects are full of suggestions for the different materials you can use to this end.

The main ways of texturing food are described in the sections below.

Powder Colours

Brushing miniature food with powder colours will give delightful results and graded effects. The following colours are the most useful:

- Burnt sienna: a reddish-brown for brushing onto bread, pastry, cooked meat joints, roast potatoes and anything else that needs to look browned in the oven or grilled.
- Ochre and dark brown: mixed in with burnt sienna for variation.
- Crimson: brushed in streaks on apples, used to blush peaches or touched into the centre of carved meat.
- Black: for bruises on bananas.

Varnish

Unappetizing as it sounds, varnish brushed selectively onto miniature food will make it look delicious! Gloss varnish makes food look greasy or wet as appropriate, but it is extremely important not to overdo it – all other foods should be left unvarnished.

- For greasy or oily effects – for example, on roasted food, such as joints of meat, potatoes; fried foods (eggs, bacon, chips and so on); and butter.
- For wet effects – for example, fruit showing inside a cut pie; cooked vegetables; jam inside a cake or in a tart; jellies, custard and blancmanges; and gravy.

If a food is glossy rather than wet or greasy, do not use varnish. Instead, rub on a little furniture polish. Apples look particularly good with polish.

Added Textures

You can add a variety of substances to polymer clay to texture it as long as the material will not rot and is completely dry. Simply dip the piece of clay into the material and knead until combined. The addition of a softening medium, like Fimo's Mix Quick, will make this easier. Some examples are:

- Semolina: for light-coloured cakes, bread, and applying as a crumb coating to fried food. Use fine-ground semolina.
- Sand: cakes and bread, crumb coatings.
- Poppy seeds: these look like currants in scones and fruit cakes.
- Ground nutmeg: add to brown clay for chocolate cake.

Surface Textures

To give the surface of miniature food a realistic texture, it can be impressed with a variety of materials, including crumpled foil, quilt wadding, sandpaper and fabric. Other suggestions are included in the projects.

Translucent Effects

Transparent clay combined with various coloured clays will give the translucent effects you need with some foods. Some examples are:

Lines of fat in sliced meat
Green grapes
Cake icings
Jams and jellies
Flesh of citrus fruits
Blancmanges and custards
Lettuce and cucumber

When you are making a particular type of food you will find it extremely helpful to have either a sample of the real thing or a colour photograph beside you as you work.

Wood

Because polymer clay can be marbled (see page 23), a variety of wood grains can be simulated. The fine lines of marbling give an excellent 1:12 scale grain and so are ideal for doll's houses.

Colour mixtures to suggest three different types of wood are given here, but do try mixing your own.

Mahogany = 3 dark brown + 1 black + 1 ochre
Oak = 3 light brown + 1 dark brown + 1 ochre
Pine = 1 ochre + 1 beige + 1 white

Marbling for Wood Grain

Make a 6mm (¼in) thick log, about 5cm (2in) long, of the main colour and logs of equal length of the remaining colours. Press them together and roll into a long 6mm (¼in) thick log. Fold this into three and roll thin again. Continue folding and rolling until the streaks of colour are 1mm (¹⁄₃₂in) thick or less, but do not continue too long or the clay will mix completely. Finally, fold into a fatter log, for rolling flat or whatever the project requires.

When you use the wood grain clay, keep the streaks aligned longitudinally, just like real wood grain, although the occasional loop looks effective.

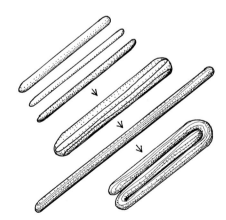

Grooving

This technique, which is used to simulate turned wood, involves making concentric grooves round a log of clay. It can also be used for metal effects.

First, make a log of clay of the required thickness. Place the log on the board horizontally and lay the side of a wool needle across it. Push the needle back and forth with a sawing motion across the log, causing the log to roll. Press down lightly, keeping the needle at right angles to the log and it will make a groove right round the log.

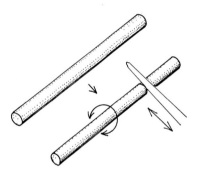

To make sharper grooves, use a darning needle or even the side of a pair of scissors if you want a squared groove. Different spacing between grooves will give different effects, very like turned wood. This method is used for the stool legs (page 109) and the Tiffany lamp (page 60) as well as in several other projects.

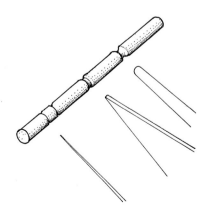

Finishes for Wood

After baking, any bubbles or irregularities can be sanded away and the piece polished (see page 20). This gives an effect similar to French polishing and makes the wood grain glow beautifully. Pine or more everyday objects can be left unpolished for a matt surface. Gloss varnish gives a shine like varnished wood. To simulate painted wood, use clay that is the colour of the paint and then varnish with gloss varnish.

Metal

Many different types of metal are simulated in the projects and the main types are given here.

- Cast iron: use black clay, apply the occasional rivet and leave any bubbles or imperfections showing for the effect of age. It can be polished for a dull shine.
- Enamelled metal: use white clay (or coloured) and apply a little black paint to edges to suggest chipping. Paint with gloss varnish.
- Brass: use white clay for new brass, dark brown for tarnished brass, and brush with metallic gold powder. Bake and apply gloss varnish. Use grooving (see page 27) for brass handles and make tiny indentations over large surfaces to look like beaten metal.
- Copper: as for brass but use copper powder or copper paint.
- Silver: use white clay for new silver and black for tarnished silver. Brush with silver powder, allowing the black to show through a little. Bake and then varnish with gloss varnish. Use stamps for worked and embossed silver.
- Gold: apply gold powder thickly to white clay. Use gloss varnish after baking.

Saucepan Formers

These are larger formers that are covered in foil and used to make saucepans and cauldrons by applying rolled-out sheets of clay.

20mm (¾in) Saucepan Former

Using scrap clay, form a 25mm (1in) ball and roll it into a short log, 20mm (¾in) thick, keeping the ends evenly rounded. To make it as round in cross section as possible, you can roll it on the board with a tile. Press one end on the board so that it is flat but still with rounded edges. Cut the other end off with a very sharp blade and roll it lightly on its side again to eliminate any flattening from the cut. Bake it standing on end for 10 minutes.

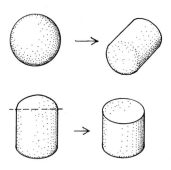

Make several other saucepan formers in larger sizes. A cauldron former needs to be about 30mm (1¼in) in diameter.

Leather and Fabric

Thinly rolled-out polymer clay can be formed into small shoes, bags and satchels like real leather. It can then be stamped and gilded as in the books project on page 56. Use muted clay colours, such as light brown, navy blue and dark red, and leave the surface matt after baking.

Real fabric is usually used for miniature fabric in the doll's house but occasionally, polymer clay simulated fabric can be very useful. To simulate a fabric, roll out the clay very thinly and then lay it on a woven fabric and roll this onto the surface so that it makes an impression. The sacks described on page 33 are made using this technique.

Plants and Flowers

Polymer clays can be used to make wonderfully realistic plants and flowers and many techniques are covered in detail in Chapter 6 and 7. The fine texture and strength of the clays means that petals and leaves can be made extremely thin and delicate.

Do not be afraid to roll the clay paper thin for petals but try to handle them as little as possible as very thin clay soon becomes limp from the heat of your hands. Use your knife or needle to position tiny pieces. Translucent clay comes into its own when used for flowers as it can be mixed with small quantities of colour to create beautiful translucent petals. Powder colour brushed onto the tips of petals is another delightful effect. Leaves can be made to look more realistic by pressing the underside of a real tiny leaf onto the clay.

When making a collection of plants that will be displayed together, vary the leaf green of the different plants for a more natural look. It is a good idea always to make a few extra flowers so that you build up a stock of different colours for future arrangements.

Fine florists' wire is often used for stems. You will need wire cutters or an old pair of scissors to cut the wire. To make a small loop at the end of a wire, such as for the roses and carnations, use a pair of fine-nosed pliers: grip the end of the wire in the pliers and rotate them to curve the wire into a loop.

Some projects use beading wire to insert into the clay to make bendable stems. This type of wire can be cut with old scissors and smoothed to the right shape in your fingers.

FOLLOWING THE INSTRUCTIONS IN THIS BOOK

All the projects are illustrated with step-by-step instructions to make them easy to follow. Measurements are given to help you to keep to the correct proportions – for example, log thickness, the diameter of balls of clay and the lengths of cut pieces of log required are given. In the case of logs, the first measurement given is always the log thickness. Keep a ruler beside you as you work so that you can refer to it for accurate sizing.

Quantities of clay required are not given in the lists of materials because all the projects will require less than one 60g (2oz) packet of clay.

CHAPTER 3

KITCHEN
MINIATURES

For good reason, the kitchen is often called the heart of the home, and it is a wonderful room to create in miniature. It provides the opportunity to make a profusion of miniatures, ranging from tiny vegetables and pies to utensils and containers of every kind.

The kitchen is a good place for a beginner to start because the projects range from the simple (breads and vegetables) right through to the more advanced (the sink and the kitchen range).

Instructions for the polymer clay miniatures in the photograph are all found in this chapter apart from the following: mantle shelf (page 119); clock (page 50); candlestick (page 52); jugs (page 89); stool (page 109); tea set (page 88); brushes (page 92); bucket (page 125); picture (page 102); tiles (page 114).

MINIATURE VEGETABLES

*Vegetables are some of the easiest miniatures to make in polymer clay,
largely because vegetables are naturally irregular, and the clay forms
easily into their rounded shapes.*

MATERIALS

Potatoes
- Polymer clay: beige, yellow
- Artist's pastel: crimson, ochre
- Cocktail stick

Carrots
- Polymer clay: orange, white
- Artist's pastel: dark green

Cabbage
- Polymer clay: leaf green, white, yellow

Cauliflower
- Polymer clay: leaf green, white, yellow, ochre
- Small piece of quilt wadding

Onions
- Polymer clay: ochre, orange, white, dark brown
- Toothbrush

MIXTURES

Potatoes
- potato flesh = 1 beige + trace of yellow

Carrots
- carrot orange = orange + trace of white

Cabbage
- marbled light green
  = 2 white + 2 leaf green + 1 yellow;
- marbled mid-green
  = 4 leaf green + 1 marbled light green

Cauliflower
- marbled mid-green as for the cabbage;
- curd white = white + trace of ochre

Onions
- onion bronze
  = 2 ochre + 1 orange + 1 white

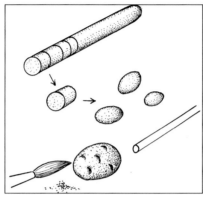

1 To make potatoes, form a log of potato flesh mixture, 6mm (¼in) thick, and cut lengths between 6mm (¼in) and 3mm (⅛in). Shape these into balls and then into ovals. Rub the crimson and ochre pastels onto a piece of paper to release some powder and brush a mixture of this all over each potato. Cut the end off a cocktail stick and rub the cut end onto the crimson powder. Mark the potatoes at intervals, with the cut edge held at an angle, to make eyes.

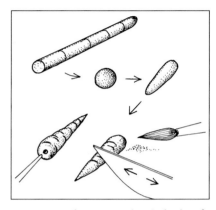

2 Form a log, 3mm (⅛in) thick, of the carrot mixture and cut lengths between 10mm (⅜in) and 13mm (½in). Form these into balls and then point one end into a carrot shape. Lay each on the board and roll under a knife blade to make little horizontal creases. Poke a hole in the tops with a wool needle and dust the tops with a little green pastel.

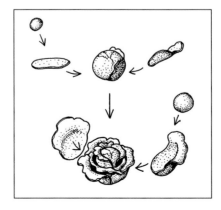

3 For the cabbage, marble the colours given above until the streaks are quite fine (see page 22). Form an 8mm (⁵⁄₁₆in) ball of the light green for the cabbage heart and mark to suggest leaves. Form several 5mm (³⁄₁₆in) balls of light green and roll them very thin. Curl the tops back and apply to the centre ball. Repeat with 6mm (¼in) balls of the mid-green for the outside leaves, applying more loosely and curving the tops back.

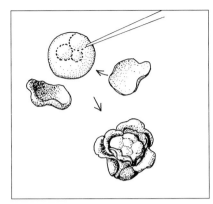

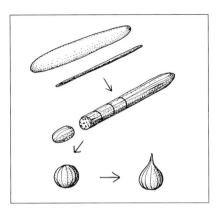

4 To make the cauliflower, form a 13mm (½in) ball of the curd white clay and prick circles with a wool needle. Press a piece of quilt wadding onto the clay to texture the curds. Now apply outer leaves as for the cabbage, turning the tops over and outwards to reveal the curds.

5 To make onions, form a log, 6mm (¼in) thick and about 5cm (2in) long, of the onion bronze and apply a log, 1.5mm (⅟₁₆in) thick, of dark brown to one side. Marble this into the clay (see page 22) until it forms thin streaks in a log 6mm (¼in) thick. Cut several 5mm (³⁄₁₆in) lengths and form into balls. Keeping the streaks aligned vertically, pinch out the top of each into a point for an onion shape.

6 Mix a little white into ochre clay, form tiny balls and press flat on the board. Texture with the toothbrush and apply with a knife to the bottom of the onion. Make small cuts in the point and give it a twist. Make a few pieces of onion skin by rolling some of the streaky bronze into petal-thin flakes, then slicing them off the board with your knife, which makes them curl.

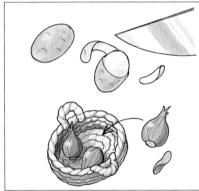

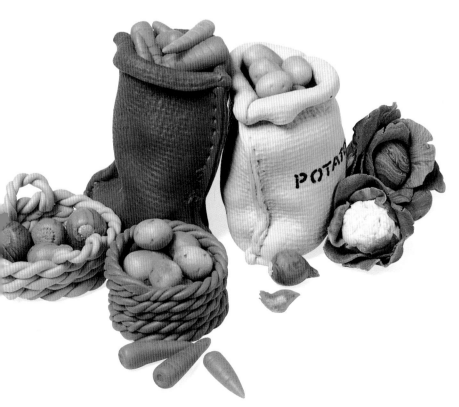

7 Bake all the vegetables for about 10 minutes. Arrange some in the baskets (see page 36) and sacks (see below). It is possible to peel the potatoes to look quite realistic. The onions should be mixed with the loose pieces of skin.

The sacks in the photograph are made from rolled-out sheets of clay that have had a piece of woven fabric pressed onto the surface.

BREAD

A loaf of bread, partly sliced, stands surrounded by some other types of loaf. Bread is fun and easy to make in a variety of shapes.

MATERIALS

- Polymer clay: white, ochre, beige, light brown
- Semolina
- Artist's pastel: ochre, burnt sienna, dark brown
- Small piece of quilt wadding
- Foil
- Matt varnish

MIXTURES

- White bread
  = 4 white + 1 ochre;
- Brown bread
  = 4 beige + 1 light brown;
- Mix semolina into the bread mixtures to texture them (see page 26)

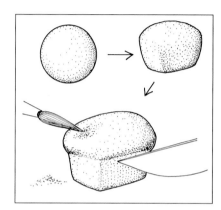

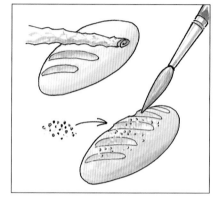

1 To make white or brown tin loaves, form the textured clay into a 20mm (¾in) ball and pinch it gently into a loaf shape, leaving the top rounded and domed. Now press the flat blade of a knife against each side to make tin marks. Rub the pastel colours onto paper and use a soft brush to brush the powder onto the bread surface – ochre all over and the browns on the top. Lightly press the quilt wadding onto the surface to texture it. Bake for 10 minutes and if you want to slice the loaf, do so before it cools.

2 To make bloomer loaves, form balls of the white, textured clay into ovals. Press the tops with quilt wadding and indent the top of each with diagonal lines using a thin roll of crumpled foil. Brush lightly with pastel colour and bake as above. When cool, brush with matt varnish and immediately sprinkle the tops with a little semolina to represent the sesame seeds.

VARIATIONS

Use the technique to make a variety of bread shapes. The cottage loaves are two balls of clay, one slightly smaller than the other which is pressed on top of the larger one. Dinner rolls and French bread could be made by the same method. Adding poppy seeds to the clay will give a currant loaf.

MINIATURE PIES

The secret of making good pies in polymer clay is to make and bake a pie dish first.
Then you can crimp the pastry lid onto the pie as in 'real' cooking.
The use of pastel colour for browning the pastry gives a realistic effect.
These instructions are for a cherry pie.

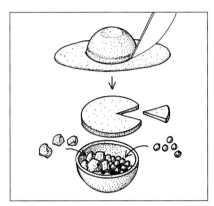

MATERIALS

- Polymer clay: beige, crimson, light brown, red, white
- 20mm (¾in) marble
- Talcum powder
- Sandpaper
- Small piece of quilt wadding
- Artist's pastel: ochre, burnt sienna
- Gloss varnish

MIXTURE

- Terracotta
  = 2 light brown + 1 red + 1 white

1 Make a pie dish with terracotta clay, following the bowl instructions on page 24. Roll out the beige clay to about 1.5mm (¹⁄₁₆in) thick. Place the bowl upside down onto the clay and cut round to make the pie crust. Cut a wedge out of the crust. Fill the pie with 1.5mm (¹⁄₁₆in) balls of crimson clay, for cherries, keeping them lower on the side that will have the wedge removed. To save time, you can fill the hidden side with cut lumps of clay. Place a few balls on top of the scraps so that they will show as bumps through the pie crust.

2 Lift the crust onto the pie, pat down and decorate the edge by pressing all round with the tip of the needle. Brush the top of the pie with ochre and burnt sienna pastel colour and make two slits. Bake for 10 minutes and when cool, drop gloss varnish onto the cherries that are visible in the pie.

VARIATIONS

You can make pies in all shapes and sizes. Try varying the filling by using different coloured clays for different fruit. You could also place meat, vegetables and gravy in the pie dish, using the instructions on page 70. A few leaf shapes cut from scraps can be used as decoration.

BASKETS

*Baskets are fun to make with polymer clay, and a good
selection of different-sized baskets has endless uses in a doll's house. In addition to
vegetable baskets, you can make laundry baskets, log baskets, sewing baskets
and picnic baskets, to name only a few.*

MATERIALS

- Polymer clay: ochre, white, light brown, dark brown, yellow
- Foil

MIXTURES

- Use any combinations of these clays to make different colours for baskets

VARIATIONS

Vary the colours of clay to add variety. Make two small lug handles for either side of a basket as shown in the photograph. Apply a rope of a different colour at any point while coiling, as in the log basket. Marbled clay can give the effect of a straw basket. You can make hinged lids for your baskets by making a flat piece for the lid in the shape of the basket bottom, piercing corresponding holes, and hinging the lid with two small pieces of wire.

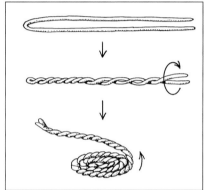

1 To make a simple oval basket, roll a log of clay, 1.5mm (¹⁄₁₆in) thick and about 10cm (4in) long. Fold double and press one end onto the board. Now twist the other end until it twines into a rope. Coil the rope, arranging the first few coils flat on the board to make an oval about 20mm (¾in) wide.

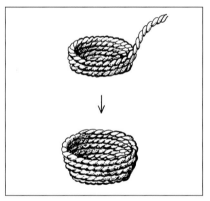

2 Begin to work up the sides, squeezing gently to secure each new coil and flaring the basket out as you go. Finish the top by trimming the rope and pressing the end down as neatly as possible.

3 For the handle, make a rope of clay and double it – it should be long enough to curve over the top of the basket. Press one end inside the basket and curve the handle over to the other side, inserting a small roll of foil under the handle to support it while it bakes. Trim the handle if necessary and press the second end inside the basket. Bake for about 15 minutes and remove the foil only when the basket is cool.

BREAD BOARD AND KNIFE

The pine bread board, carved with leaves, is redolent of country kitchens and home-made bread. The bread knife often had a matching wooden handle.

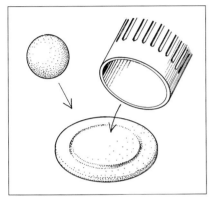

MATERIALS
- Polymer clay: ochre, beige, white
- Ceramic tile
- Cap of a large marker pen about 20mm (¾in) in diameter
- Talcum powder
- Leaf stamp (see page 19)
- Pin
- Acrylic paint: silver

MIXTURE
- Pine wood grain see page 27

1 Form a 15mm (⅝in) ball of the pine clay and press onto the tile, keeping the 'wood grain' in attractive lines. Press with your fingers until it forms a circle of clay, a little more than 25mm (1in) across. Mark a circle around the edge by pressing on the cap of a large marker pen or similar cap.

2 Brush the rim of the board with talc and decorate it by impressing it with a leaf stamp. Mark vertical lines to divide the decoration and, if you wish, you can write 'BREAD' in one of the spaces. Leave on the tile for baking.

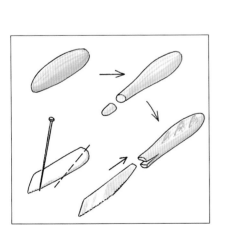

3 Form a short log of the marbled clay, 5mm (³⁄₁₆in) thick, thin one end slightly and trim to 15mm (⅝in) thick. Form a log, 3mm (⅛in) long, of white and roll flat. Cut this into a knife blade shape, thin the cutting edge and mark serrations with a pin. Make a cut in the thinner end of the handle and insert the end of the blade. Mark a design on the handle with the stamp. Bake the pieces on the tile for 20 minutes. When cool, paint the knife blade silver.

MIXING BOWL, SPOONS AND ROLLING PIN

The large creamware mixing bowl is practically an institution in British kitchens and is still used today. Wooden spoons and a traditional rolling pin complete the picture.

MATERIALS
- Polymer clay: ochre, white, beige, golden-yellow
- Talcum powder
- 6mm (¼in) former (see page 24)
- 22mm (⅞in) marble
- Paper clip
- Sandpaper
- Acrylic paint: white
- Gloss varnish

MIXTURES
- Pine wood grain see page 27;
- Creamware
  = 4 white + 2 ochre + 1 golden-yellow

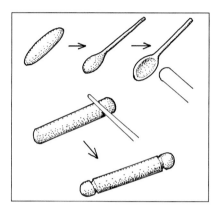

1 Make wooden spoons from logs of marbled pine clay that have had one end thinned into a handle. Press the rounded end of the former onto the other end to make a spoon bowl.

The rolling pin is simply a pine log that has had the ends grooved (see page 27). Alternatively, glue two oval handles onto a log of pine after baking.

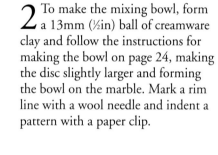

2 To make the mixing bowl, form a 13mm (½in) ball of creamware clay and follow the instructions for making the bowl on page 24, making the disc slightly larger and forming the bowl on the marble. Mark a rim line with a wool needle and indent a pattern with a paper clip.

3 Flatten a 6mm (¼in) ball of clay into a disc 10mm (⅜in) across and apply it to the base of the bowl. Bake for 10 minutes on the marble. When cool, sand away any bumps in the rim by rubbing the upturned bowl on sandpaper. Apply several coats of white acrylic paint to the inside of the bowl. When the paint is completely dry, varnish the bowl inside and out.

STORAGE JARS

Jars, jugs, crocks and basins are all part of the homely tradition of pottery in the kitchen. These little storage jars can also be made in terracotta-coloured clay for a traditional look.

MATERIALS

- Polymer clay: beige
- Talcum powder
- Wool needle and paintbrush handles for potting (see page 25)
- Small pen cap or drinking straw
- Sandpaper
- Acrylic paint: dark brown
- Gloss varnish
- Fine pen and Indian ink

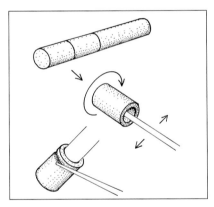

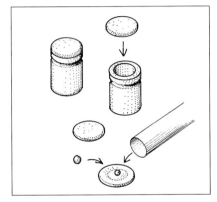

1 For the storage jars, form a log, 10mm (⅜in) thick, of beige clay and cut several lengths each about 13mm (½in) long. If the cutting distorts the cylinders, roll them lightly on the board. Pierce the centre of a cylinder with a wool needle and follow the instructions on page 25 for 'potting' the clay, keeping the sides as vertical as possible. When the sides of the jar are about 1.5mm (1/16in) thick, insert a thin pencil to support the sides and mark a rim with the side of a wool needle. Repeat for the other jars, making them in different sizes. Bake the jars for 10 minutes.

2 To make the lids, flatten small balls of clay onto the board until they are just less than the diameter of the jars. Press one gently onto each jar to seat it and remove carefully. Impress each with a small pen cap or drinking straw to make a ring and apply a tiny ball of clay for the handle. Bake the lids for 10 minutes.

3 Brush the jars and lids with nail varnish remover to de-grease them, and paint the lids and the rims of the jars with dark brown paint. When the paint is dry, varnish the paint only, leaving the beige areas matt.

Write SUGAR or TEA or whatever you wish on the sides of the jars using a fine pen and Indian ink.

VARIATIONS

The shelves pictured on page 31 show what a variety of crockery can be made from the basic instructions throughout this book. The jugs have been made in various sizes from the instructions on page 89 and painted with different designs. The mugs are made in the same way as the storage jars above, with handles added.

COPPER POTS AND PANS

These traditional cooking utensils are often displayed as ornaments in today's kitchens but were used universally by wealthier Victorian households. If you want to make more humble cast-iron pots for your doll's house kitchen, omit the copper powder.

MATERIALS
- Polymer clay: black
- Assorted saucepan formers (see page 28)
- Foil
- Metallic powder or acrylic paint: copper
- Gloss varnish
- Pen cap

1 To make a basic saucepan, first cover a 13mm (½in) former with foil. Smooth the foil down as much as possible by rubbing it with the back of a spoon. Roll out the black clay until it is 1.5mm (¹⁄₁₆in) thick, place the former on the clay and cut round it to make the pot base. Press the base onto the bottom of the former, neatening the edges.

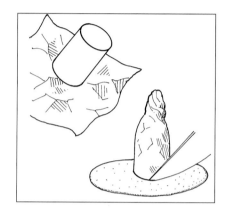

VARIATIONS

You can make a selection of saucepans, pans and cauldrons by varying the size of the former. Lids are made as for the storage jar lids on page 39. Two-handled pots are made by omitting the single handle and applying two thin logs of clay to the opposite sides of the pot.

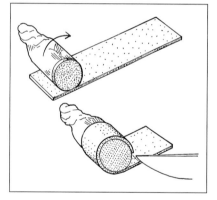

2 Cut a strip of clay, 13mm (½in) wide and about 7.5cm (3in) long, from the clay sheet and slice under it to free it from the board. Lay the former on its side on the strip with the base aligned with the edge. Roll the former up in the strip until the beginning of the strip makes a mark on the clay. Unwind a little and cut along the mark. This should ensure that the two edges meet exactly. Smooth out the joins and trim the top edge.

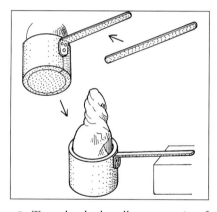

3 To make the handle, cut a strip of clay about 25mm (1in) long and 3mm (⅛in) wide. Press one end on to the pan side and apply some tiny slices of a very thin log for rivets. Bend the handle down into a right angle. Brush all over with copper powder. Support the handle with a block of clay that has been covered in foil and bake for 20 minutes. Remove the former from inside the foil and then pull the foil out of the pot. Varnish with gloss varnish.

4 To make the kettle, form a 15mm (⅝in) ball of black clay. Roll gently on its side on the board to make the sides more upright and press lightly onto the board to flatten the bottom. Indent the top with a pen cap to suggest a lid and press on a tiny ball for a lid handle.

5 Roll a log, 3mm (⅛in) thick, of black and taper one end to a point. Cut a V-shape out of the point. Cut at an angle 20mm (¾in) from the point. Press the spout onto the kettle and curve the end. Form a log, 3mm (⅛in) thick, of black for the handle, flatten it slightly and cut a 35mm (1⅜in) length. Apply to the top and press on a short log of black clay on top. Brush with copper powder, leaving the handle top black. Bake as above and varnish.

KITCHEN RANGE

Black polymer clay that is left unvarnished looks remarkably like cast iron, and the occasional blemish or wavy edge only adds to the effect of age. This project demonstrates how simple it is to cut out clay shapes and assemble them into a free-standing miniature. The range has hinged hob covers and oven door using clay to make the hinges.

MATERIALS

- Polymer clay: black, orange, yellow
- Tracing paper and pencil
- Ceramic tiles
- 13mm (½in) former (see page 24)
- Pen cap
- Pins (brass lace-making pins look best)
- Sandpaper
- Set square
- Superglue
- Wire cutters or cutting pliers

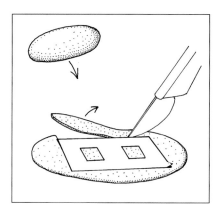

1 Trace the templates onto tracing paper and cut them out. Roll out the black clay on a tile until it is 1.5mm (1⁄16in) thick and as even as possible. Lay the traced stove front template onto the clay and cut out with a craft knife. To avoid distorting the shapes, do not move the cut-out piece, simply remove the surrounding clay. Repeat for the range top, back, base and two sides, using extra tiles if necessary.

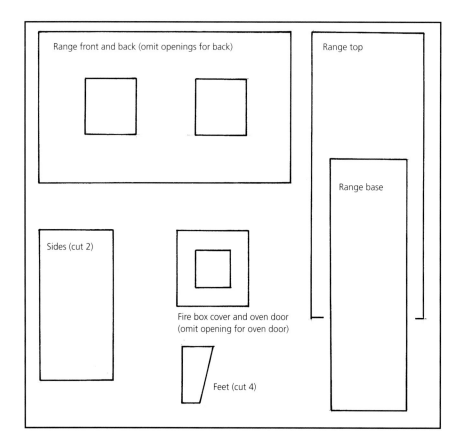

Range front and back (omit openings for back)

Range top

Range base

Sides (cut 2)

Fire box cover and oven door (omit opening for oven door)

Feet (cut 4)

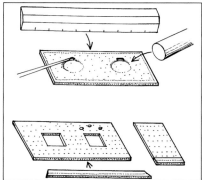

2 Indent the edges of the range top with the edge of a ruler and make two impressions with a large former for the hotplates. Make an indentation at the back of each hotplate for the hob cover hinges. Apply strips of clay, 5mm (3⁄8in) wide, along the base of the back, front and side pieces, cutting the front and back strips at an angle and marking them with a ruler as an edging. Apply some small log slices to the range front for rivets. Bake all the pieces on the tiles for 30 minutes.

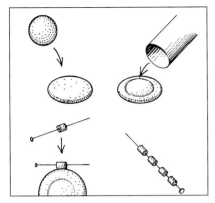

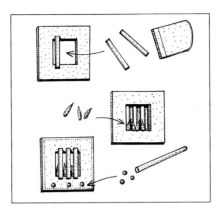

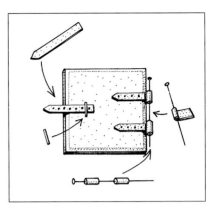

3 Form two 10mm (⅜in) balls of clay for the hob covers and press them flat onto the board until they are about 15mm (⅝in) in diameter. Indent each with the pen cap to decorate. Form a log, 1.5mm (¹⁄₁₆in) thick, and cut six 3mm (⅛in) lengths. Pierce one with a pin and, with the pin still in place, press it against the side of a cover. Repeat for the second cover. Thread the remaining four lengths onto a pin and set aside for baking.

4 Cut out the oven door and firebox cover from a clay sheet 1.5mm (¹⁄₁₆in) thick. Apply several strips of clay as bars to the firebox cover, turn the cover over and apply some small slices of orange and yellow clay to the back of the bars to represent the fire. Turn back over, mark decorative lines along the edges with the side of a needle and apply some small slices of log for rivets. Let the bars bend slightly as though they have had years of use.

5 Mark the oven door edges with lines. Cut three thin strips of black for the catch and hinge ends. Cut one end of each into a point and press them onto the oven door, making a row of holes for rivets. Press a thin bar across the catch strip. Form two small logs of clay and pierce with a pin. Press these against the side of the door, 6mm (¼in) apart. Roll another pin in a strip of clay, just wide enough to fit between the two hinges.

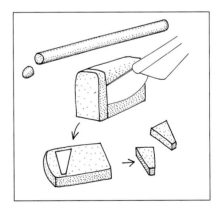

6 Make a stove pipe from a log 6mm (¼in) thick. To make the range feet, cut a slice, 5mm (³⁄₁₆in) thick, from an unkneaded block of black clay and use the template to cut out the feet. Bake all the pieces for 15 minutes.

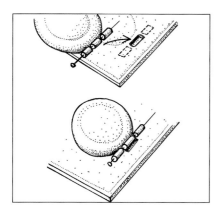

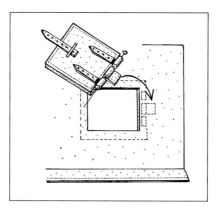

8 Assemble the oven door hinges onto one pin and trim the pin to size. Hold the door on the front of the range and check that the hinge is free to move. If necessary, cut small indentations in the range front for the outer hinges to move in. Glue the central hinge to the range front. To make the door stay shut, apply a small chip of baked clay to the front where the door shuts so that the friction holds it closed.

7 Remove the pins from the hob cover hinge parts and assemble each hob cover onto a single pin. Hold the pin in place on the range top with the central hinge in the indent to the back of the hob ring. Check that the hinge can move freely. If not, trim the clay as necessary. Cut off the ends of the pins. Apply glue to the two outside hinges and press onto the range top so that the central hinge seats in the indent.

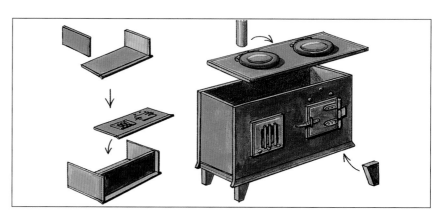

9 To assemble the range, lay the back on the board and glue the sides to it, using a set square to keep the sides vertical and aligning the bases. Glue the base to the back and sides, just above the bottom strips, again ensuring it is vertical. Glue on the front and finally, the top, trimming or sanding any edges that are not straight. Glue the wedge feet to the bottom of the range and glue the stove pipe to the top.

KITCHEN SINK

This project is for an unglazed pottery kitchen sink that was typically found in country kitchens and sculleries in the nineteenth century. It is supported on 'brick' piers and has a single tap and a plug.

MATERIALS

- Polymer clay: ochre, beige, white, black
- Cardboard soap carton (125g/4½oz size is ideal), wrapped neatly in foil with the ends taped down
- Ceramic tile
- Sandpaper
- Small piece of quilt wadding
- Silver-plated jewellery chain, 50mm (2in) long
- 2 silver-plated peg-and-loop jewellery findings (see page 16)
- Superglue and PVA glue
- Acrylic paint: silver, brick red, brown, white
- Tracing paper and pencil
- Cocktail stick
- Air-drying clay

MIXTURES

- Cream = 2 ochre + 1 white; You will need the equivalent of about half a 60g/2oz packet;
- For pine wood grain see page 27

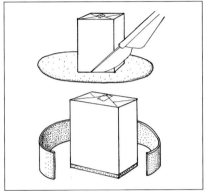

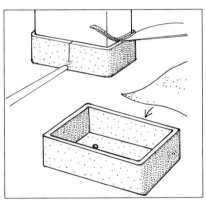

1 Roll out one half of the cream mixture to a little under 3mm (⅛in) thick. Place the end of the prepared carton onto the clay and cut around it for the sink base. Roll out the remaining cream clay to the same thickness and cut a strip 20mm (¾in) wide and long enough to wrap round the carton, covering the clay base. Trim the edges neatly where they overlap so that the two ends butt together.

2 Smooth the joins into the clay and trim off the top of the sink if necessary to ensure a straight top edge. Any small blemishes can be sanded down after baking. Make a drainage hole in the base of the sink with a point. Bake the sink for 20 minutes. When still slightly warm, remove from the carton. Sand the sink to remove any bumps and sand the top edges into a curve. Rub the surface with quilt wadding to give a shine (see page 20).

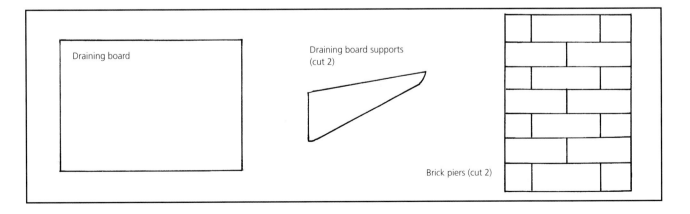

Draining board

Draining board supports (cut 2)

Brick piers (cut 2)

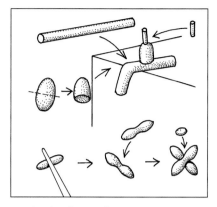

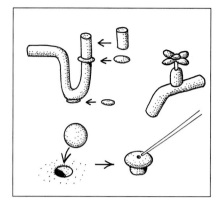

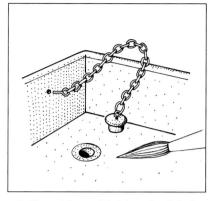

3 Make the tap by cutting a piece 20mm (¾in) long from a 3mm (⅛in) thick log of black clay. Place this so that it hangs over the edge of the foil-covered soap carton. Form a 6mm (¼in) oval of clay, cut off the base and apply it to the tap. Cut a 3mm (⅛in) length of a log, 1.5mm (⅟₁₆in) thick, and apply it to the top. Make the tap top by forming two small ovals, 5mm (³⁄₁₆in) long, and grooving their centres (see page 27). Press the ovals together and press a small disc of white clay on top. (The top will be glued to the tap after baking to avoid distortion.)

4 Make a waste pipe by curving a length of log, 5mm (³⁄₁₆in) thick, into the shape shown and applying discs of clay for fittings. Form a 3mm (⅛in) ball of clay for the plug and press into the hole in the sink to shape it. Make a small hole in the top of the plug. Bake the plumbing for about 10 minutes. Glue the top onto the tap.

5 Cut a 25mm (1in) length of chain and attach each end to a peg and loop fitting. Heat the point of a needle over a flame and make a small hole in the end of the sink for the plug chain attachment. Using Superglue, glue in one peg and loop fitting and glue the other into the hole in the plug. Paint the tap, the waste pipe and a ring round the plug hole with silver paint.

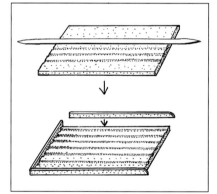

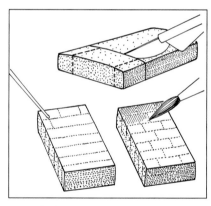

6 Trace and cut out the draining board and support templates. Roll out the pine clay on the tile into a sheet, 3mm (⅛in) thick, and cut out the board and supports. Trim the board, if necessary, to fit the sink. Mark regular grooves in the board with the side of a cocktail stick. Roll out some more of the pine clay until it is 1.5mm (⅟₁₆in) thick and cut strips to apply with your knife to the sides of the board. Bake on the tile for 20 minutes.

7 The brick piers are made with air-drying modelling clay to give a coarser texture. The clay comes in slabs about 13mm (½in) thick, so simply cut the piers directly from this, using the template. Mark bricks by pressing the edge of a ruler horizontally against the clay and marking vertical lines with a point. Allow to dry for 24 hours and then paint with a varied mixture of brick red, brown and white acrylic paint and leaving the lines between the bricks unpainted.

8 Using PVA glue, fix the sink onto the brick supports against a wall in your doll's house kitchen. Trim the waste pipe and glue into place with Superglue. Glue the supports to the side of the sink and the draining board on top, overhanging the sink slightly. Trim the tap if necessary and glue it as if it is coming out of the wall above the sink.

The instructions for the tiles in the photograph are on page 114.

CHAPTER 4

LIVING ROOM MINIATURES

The doll's house living room can be designed as a homely family room, an elegant drawing room or something entirely different. The decoration and miniatures need to be chosen to reflect not only the period but the style, and this is one of the delights of creating miniature rooms.

The projects given here are mostly for classic pieces of the Victorian and Edwardian eras, but many can be adapted to fit into earlier or later periods. Suggestions for variations are included with many of the projects.

All the polymer clay miniatures in the photograph are projects in this chapter apart from: the double shelf, (page 119); plates (page 64); vases (page 98); pictures (page 102); cup and saucer (page 88); sewing things (page 100); basket (page 36); aspidistra (page 80); trailing plant (page 84); flowers (page 94-97).

MANTELPIECE CLOCK

*This project uses unkneaded blocks of clay to provide the basic shape,
which is then veneered to simulate a wooden case clock.*

MATERIALS

- Polymer clay: dark brown, black, ochre, white
- Tracing paper and pencil
- Pen cap
- Acrylic paint: gold
- Optional paper clock face (see page 16) or black acrylic paint
- Sandpaper
- Matt varnish
- Gloss varnish

MIXTURES

- Mahogany wood grain see page 27

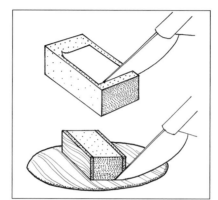

1 Trace and cut out the templates. Cut a slice, 10mm (⅜in) thick, from an unkneaded block of dark brown clay and use the template to cut out the clock body. Roll out the mahogany clay into a sheet about 1.5mm (¹⁄₁₆in) thick and use this to cover the sides and then the front of the block. To veneer each surface, hold the block onto the rolled-out clay and cut round neatly. Slice under the clay and smooth the veneer firmly on.

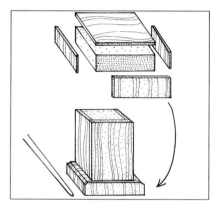

2 Cut a 3mm (⅛in) slice from the unkneaded dark brown clay and cut out the clock base. Veneer the sides, top and front in that order. Press the clock onto the base and indent the two sides of the base with the side of a wool needle. Stroke all over the surface of the veneer to remove fingerprints and avoid touching it with your fingers from now on.

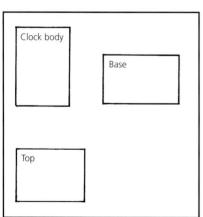

```
Clock body

        Base

Top
```

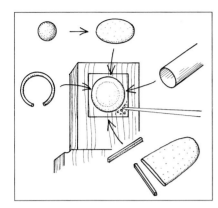
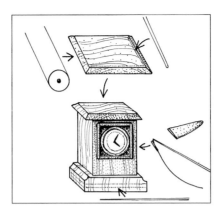

3 Lay the clock on its back to continue. Form a 5mm (³⁄₁₆in) ball of white clay and flatten on the board into a disc 10mm (⅜in) across. Indent this with a pen cap or similar marking tool. Slice off the board and carefully apply to the front of the clock. Form a log, 1mm (¹⁄₃₂in) thick, of dark brown and use to ring the clock face, placing the join at the bottom. Mark a square around the face and use the tip of a wool needle to impress a pattern. Cut thin strips of mahogany and apply to the sides of the square.

4 Roll out a small sheet of mahogany, 2mm (just over ¹⁄₁₆in) thick, and cut out the clock top. Press the side of a pencil against each side to chamfer it. Press the side of a wool needle just inside the chamfered edge to accentuate it. Slice off the board and press gently on the top of the clock. Cut two thin slices of black and apply with your knife to the face for the hands (unless you are using a paper face). Mark the base with horizontal lines using the side of a needle.

5 Bake the clock for 15 minutes. Paint the area inside the square with gold paint. Glue on a paper clock face, if using, otherwise mark small spots of black paint round the face for numbers. Sand and polish any irregularities if necessary (see page 20), and apply a coat of matt varnish to the mahogany clay. Varnish the face with gloss varnish.

CANDLESTICKS

These low candlesticks are the sort that Victorians carried up to bed. They can also be brushed with silver powder to simulate silver or made with coloured clay and the edges blackened slightly to represent worn enamel. Omit the handles and make the uprights taller for the more elegant design shown on page 63.

MATERIALS

- Polymer clay: dark brown, transparent, yellow
- Pen cap
- 6mm (¼in) former (see page 24)
- Metallic powder: gold
- Gloss varnish
- Superglue

MIXTURES

- Tallow = transparent + trace of yellow

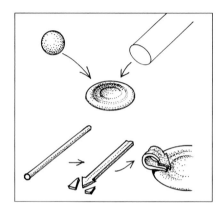

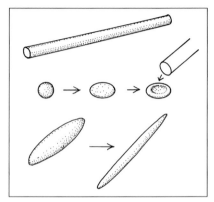

1 Form two 8mm (⁵⁄₁₆in) balls of dark brown clay and press them down onto the board to make discs about 13mm (½in) across. Indent each with a pen cap and the centre with the former. Make a log, 1.5mm (¹⁄₁₆in) thick, of dark brown and roll it flat with a pencil. Trim to an arrow shape, 13mm (½in) long, and mark a line down the centre. Press the straight end onto the base and curve the pointed end over. Repeat for the other candlestick.

2 Make a log of dark brown clay just under 3mm (⅛in) thick and about 40mm (1½in) long. Try to keep it as round in section as possible and place on the baking sheet. Cut two 3mm (⅛in) pieces from a 3mm (⅛in) thick log, form into balls and press flat on the board to make 8mm (⁵⁄₁₆in) discs. Impress with the former. Form the tallow clay into a log just thinner than the uprights and 25mm (1in) long, and taper both ends. Brush all the pieces except the candles with gold powder.

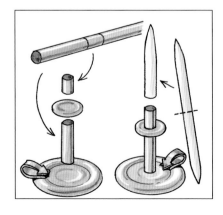

3 Bake the pieces for 10 minutes. When cool, varnish all the gold pieces. Cut two uprights, each 10mm (⅜in) long, from the baked log, ensuring you cut cleanly and straight across or the upright will tilt. Glue these to the centres of the bases. Glue on the small discs and, finally, a 3mm (⅛in) piece of the log. Cut the candle log in half and glue on top.

FOOTSTOOL

Small items of furniture are easy to make with polymer clay, particularly those incorporating curved wooden shapes. This little footstool combines polymer clay 'mahogany' with upholstery to great effect.

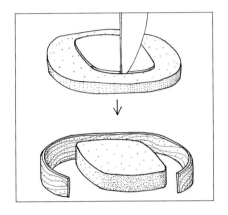

1 Trace the template and cut it out in stiff card. Roll out a small sheet of dark brown clay, 5mm (³/₁₆in) thick, on the tile. Lay on the template and cut round it, keeping your knife as vertical as possible. Remove the excess clay. Roll out some mahogany clay, 1.5mm (¹/₁₆in) thick, and cut a strip 6mm x 12cm (¼ x 5in), using a ruler to help keep the edges straight. Wrap this strip round the stool base, butting the ends and smoothing the join.

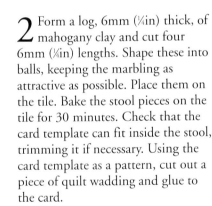

2 Form a log, 6mm (¼in) thick, of mahogany clay and cut four 6mm (¼in) lengths. Shape these into balls, keeping the marbling as attractive as possible. Place them on the tile. Bake the stool pieces on the tile for 30 minutes. Check that the card template can fit inside the stool, trimming it if necessary. Using the card template as a pattern, cut out a piece of quilt wadding and glue to the card.

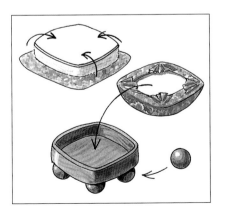

3 Cut out a piece of fabric, 6mm (¼in) larger all round than the template, and stretch this over the wadding, gluing it to the back of the card all round with PVA glue. Glue the upholstered card into the footstool. Glue the four ball feet to the bottom of the footstool with Superglue. Varnish the clay with gloss varnish.

MATERIALS

- Polymer clay: dark brown, black, ochre
- Tracing paper and pencil
- Card
- Ceramic tile
- Small piece of quilt wadding
- Cotton fabric
- Superglue and PVA glue
- Gloss varnish

MIXTURES

- Mahogany wood grain see page 27

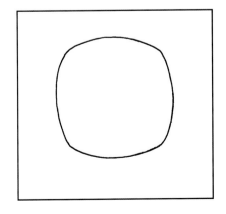

COAL SCUTTLE AND FIRESIDE TOOLS

Brass coal scuttles and sets of fireside tools are as popular today as they were in the nineteenth century. The little scuttle has a simulated beaten brass patina while the tools are decorated with a stamped maple leaf design.

MATERIALS

Coal Scuttle
- Polymer clay: dark brown
- 20mm (¾in) marble
- Small marble
- Metallic powder: gold
- Gloss varnish
- Superglue

Fireside Tools
- Polymer clay: dark brown
- Pin
- 6mm (¼in) former (see page 24)
- Small maple leaf stamp (see page 19)
- Pen cap
- Metallic powder: gold
- Gloss varnish
- Superglue

1 Roll out a sheet of dark brown clay, 1.5mm (¹⁄₁₆in) thick, and cut a strip 2 x 10cm (¾ x 4in). Wrap this around the 20mm (¾in) marble and trim the edges so they meet in a neat join. Smooth the join. Mould the clay around the marble to shape it and turn the top edge out slightly. Pull the side away from the join out into a broad lip.

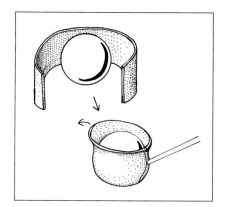

2 Flatten a 10mm (⅜in) ball of clay into a disc 15mm (⅝in) wide and apply it to the bottom of the scuttle, smoothing the join. Using the small marble, make little dents all over the sides of the scuttle to simulate beaten brass. Brush all over with gold powder, bake for 15 minutes and when it is just cool enough to handle, prize out the marble. You may have to cut neatly down the join to release it, but the cut can be glued back. Varnish the powder.

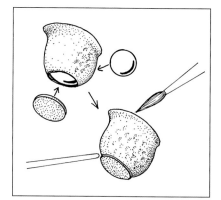

3 Form a log, 3mm (⅛in) thick, of clay and curve it over the top of the scuttle. Trim to size and flatten the ends against the sides of the scuttle. Apply two small balls to the flattened ends for rivets. Remove the handle for baking, retaining the curve. Form a thin log for the rear handle and curve into shape. Brush the pieces with gold powder and bake for 10 minutes.

Varnish the two handles and glue in place. Tiny pieces of real coal are most effective displayed inside the scuttle.

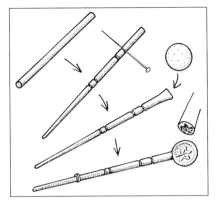

4 To make the poker, form a log, 2mm (just over 1/16in) thick, of dark brown. Trim to 50mm (2in) long and point one end. Make grooves along the poker with a pin (see page 27). Wrap a tiny strip round the poker 13mm (1/2in) above the point. Form a 3mm (1/8in) ball of clay and flatten onto the board to make a disc 8mm (5/16in) across. Flatten the top of the poker and press the disc onto it. Impress the disc with the maple leaf stamp.

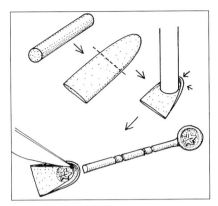

5 For the shovel, form a 6mm (1/4in) thick log with a rounded end and roll flat on the board. Trim to 20mm (3/4in) from the rounded end. Place the former just inside the rounded end and push the edges up against it. Push up the two sides against the knife blade. Stamp a leaf. Make the handle as for the poker, but 45mm (1 3/4in) long. Cut the end at an angle and push it against the rounded end of the shovel.

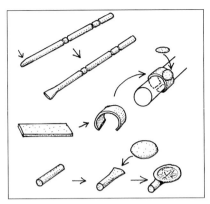

6 Make the two tong arms as for the poker but omitting the disc tops, and flatten the ends by pressing on the board. Trim to 40mm (1 1/2in) long. Roll out a small sheet of clay, 1mm (1/32in) thick, and cut a strip 20mm (3/4in) long and 5mm (3/16in) wide. Wrap this round the former and trim so that the ends do not quite meet. Apply a tiny disc to the side away from the opening. Do not remove the former until after baking. Make a decorative top as shown.

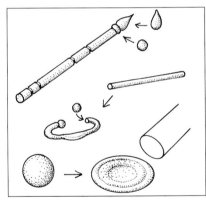

7 For the stand, make a grooved upright 3mm (1/8in) thick and 50mm (2in) long. Apply a small ball of clay and a pointed oval to the top. Form a 1.5mm (1/16in) thick log, trim it to 30mm (1 1/4in) long and flatten the centre. Apply two small balls to the ends and bend them inwards. Form a 10mm (3/8in) ball and flatten into a disc 20mm (3/4in) across. Impress with a pen cap and former.

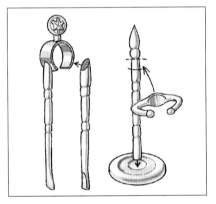

8 Brush all the pieces with gold powder and bake for 10 minutes. Varnish all the pieces.
    To assemble the tongs, glue the arms to the ring, cutting the top of the arms at an angle. Glue on the top.
    To assemble the stand, glue the flat part of the arms to the upright. Trim the bottom of the upright to level it and glue it to the centre of the base.

BOOKSHELF AND BOOKS

This project shows you how to make real little books with paper pages. The tooled effect is achieved by stamping the clay and then gilding with gold acrylic paint. The bookshelf is made in simulated mahogany with 'carved' fleur-de-lis on the ends, but you can use a stamp made from any charm.

MATERIALS

- Polymer clay: dark brown, ochre, black, assorted colours (red, navy blue, white) for the book covers
- Tracing paper and pencil
- Ceramic tile
- Small charm stamps (see page 20)
- Sandpaper
- Superglue
- Small piece of quilt wadding
- Thin paper (airmail letter paper is ideal)
- Bulldog clip
- PVA glue
- Fabric tape
- Steel rule
- Craft knife or Stanley knife
- Tooling stamps (see page 20)
- Acrylic paint: gold
- Stretch fabric sticking plaster
- Acrylic paint to match the book covers

MIXTURES

- Mahogany wood grain see page 27

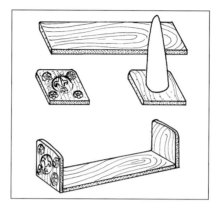

1 To make the bookshelf, trace and cut out the bookcase templates. Roll out the mahogany clay to 1.5mm (⅟₁₆in) thick on the tile and use the templates to cut out the pieces, removing the waste clay from around them. Stamp the ends with the stamps to suggest carvings. Bake the pieces on the tile for 30 minutes. When cool, sand any rough edges, glue the ends onto the base and polish with the wadding.

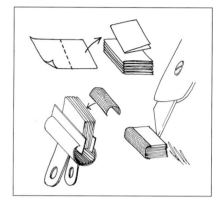

2 To make the books, use the pages template to cut 16 pieces from thin paper. Fold each piece in half, pile together and clamp in a bulldog clip with the folded ends protruding. Apply PVA glue thickly to the folded ends and then glue a piece of fabric tape, cut to size, over them. Leave to dry thoroughly. Lay the pages on a piece of board or a cutting mat and, using a steel rule as an edge, cut down with a sharp knife to trim the edges of the pages.

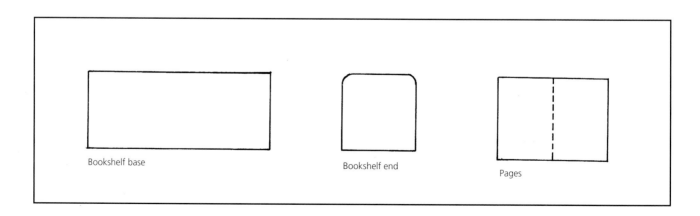

Bookshelf base

Bookshelf end

Pages

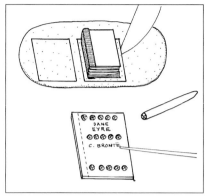

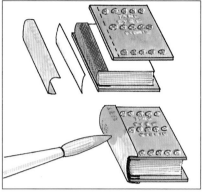

Make books in the different coloured clays suggested. The marbled book is made by marbling earth-colour clays and rolling this out into a sheet for the cover. Some of the books in the photograph are simply a complete cover, made in the same way but including a tooled spine, wrapped round a block of white clay. These are quick and easy to make to fill bookshelves.

3 Roll out a sheet of coloured clay 1mm (1⁄32in) thick on the tile and, using the trimmed pages as a guide, cut two covers slightly larger than the pages and remove the surrounding clay. Lightly stamp a pattern onto the front cover with the tooling stamps, making lines of impressions. Using a blunt wool needle, write on the name of the book or suggest a title with a row of little lines. (Remember to leave a strip undecorated for the tape.)

4 Bake the covers on the tile for 20 minutes. To gild the lettering, work some gold paint into the letters with a brush and immediately wipe over the cover with a damp cloth to remove excess paint. Apply glue to the outer pages and press the two covers onto them. Cut a piece of sticking plaster big enough to wrap round the spine and stick it in place. A piece of paper, the width of the spine, stuck inside the plaster spine will give it more shape. Paint the spine with acrylic paint to match the cover.

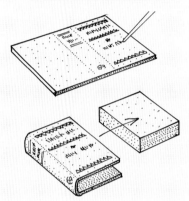

SILVER DESK SET

Desk sets were very popular in Victorian times and this miniature version uses glass beads for the ink bottles. A tiny feather makes a perfect quill pen.

MATERIALS

- Polymer clay: black, dark brown
- Ceramic tile
- Tracing paper and pencil
- Any small stamps (see pages 19-20)
- Metallic powder: silver
- Gloss varnish
- Superglue
- 2 cylindrical glass beads about 10mm (⅜in) long and 8mm (⁵⁄₁₆in) in diameter
- Small feather

1 For the blotter, form a log, 15mm (⅝in) thick, of dark brown and cut an 8mm (⁵⁄₁₆in) slice. Cut this in half for the blotter base. Roll out black clay to 1.5mm (¹⁄₁₆in) thick and use the template to cut out the blotter top. Stamp a design and indent the edge. Flatten a 3mm (⅛in) ball of black clay into a disc, apply a short length of 3mm (⅛in) thick log and then press on another small ball. Press the handle onto the centre of the blotter top.

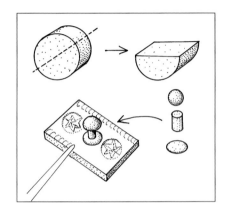

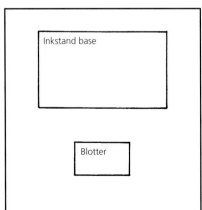

2 Dust the top with silver powder and bake the two pieces for 20 minutes. Varnish with gloss varnish. Cut a piece of paper the same width as the blotter base and long enough to curve round and over the top on each side. Glue in place and glue the top over it.

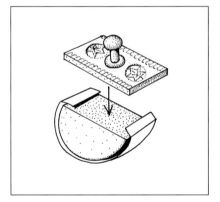

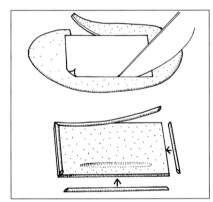

3 To make the inkstand, trace and cut out the template. Roll out the black clay on the tile into a sheet 1.5mm (¹⁄₁₆in) thick and use the template to cut out the stand base. Remove the surrounding clay and mark a pen slot with the side of a wool needle. Form a thin log of clay, about 1mm (¹⁄₃₂in) thick and 15cm (6in) long, and apply all round the edge of the stand, mitring the corners.

Inkstand base

Blotter

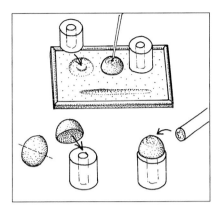

4 Place the two beads upright on the stand and press down to make an indentation for each. Form a 6mm (¼in) ball of black clay and cut it in half. Press one half onto the top of each bead and impress with one of the small stamps to decorate. Press another half ball onto the space between the ink pots for the pen holder, stamp and then make a small hole to take the quill.

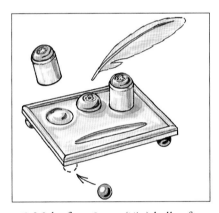

5 Make four 3mm (⅛in) balls of black clay for the feet and brush all the clay with silver powder. Bake the stand on the tile with the other pieces for 30 minutes. Slice the stand off the tile and varnish all the silver parts. Glue the ball feet to the corners of the underside of the stand. Push the feather into the hole in the pen holder.

TIFFANY-STYLE LAMP

There is something magical about miniature lighting, and polymer clay is an excellent material for making lamps that are quite easy to electrify. The Tiffany shade requires a steady hand, but the results are delightful when the lamp is lit! For an easier fabric lampshade see page 99.

For an easier fabric lampshade see page 99.

MATERIALS

- Polymer clay: dark brown, turquoise, transparent, black
- Tracing paper and pencil
- Stiff card that can be curved without creasing
- Cocktail stick
- 13mm (½in) and 6mm (¼in) formers (see page 24)
- Doll's house light bulb with attached wire and plug (see page 16)
- Glass paints: red, green, yellow (see page 14)
- Matt varnish
- Gloss varnish
- Superglue

MIXTURES

- Bronze = 2 dark brown + 1 turquoise

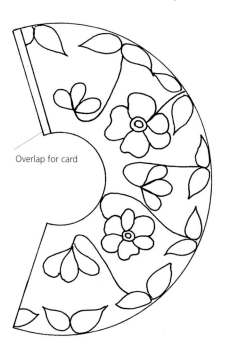

Overlap for card

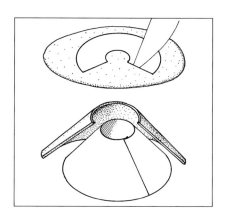

1 Trace the lampshade template onto the card and cut out. Roll out a sheet of transparent clay to 1mm (¹⁄₃₂in) thick, and use the template to cut out the shade. Now curve the card template into a shade and glue the ends together. Lift the cut-out clay shape onto the card shade, trim to fit and smooth the edges together so that the clay is supported by its shape in card.

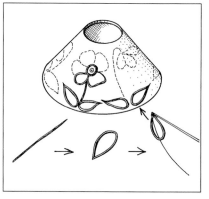

2 Form black clay into 1mm (¹⁄₃₂in) thick logs or wires of clay about 20mm (¾in) long. Form these into leaf shapes on the board by curving the ends round and pressing them together into a point. Lift them onto the shade with your knife, applying leaves all round the bottom in pairs, using the template as a guide. The drooping poppies are simply leaf shapes clustered together and the open poppies are small circles with irregular petals all round.

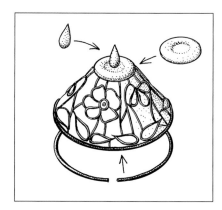

3 When all the flowers and leaves are in place, apply further wires of clay, imitating stained glass and making irregular vertical lines. Finally, apply a slightly thicker log all round the bottom edge. Form a 10mm (⅜in) ball of bronze clay and flatten into a 15mm (⅝in) disc. Impress the centre with a former and apply a small oval, shaped into a point at one end, for a finial. Bake the shade for 10 minutes and when cool, ease it off the card. Glue the disc to the top.

60

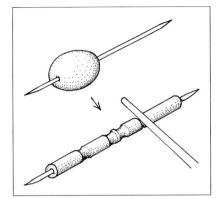

4 Using the bronze clay, form a 20mm (¾in) ball and pierce it through the middle with the cocktail stick. Roll the ball with the cocktail stick inside on the board so that it forms a log round the cocktail stick. If it begins to loosen around the stick, squeeze it back on. The log should be about 50mm (2in) long and 6mm (¼in) thick. Use a paint-brush handle to groove the log (see page 27). Leave the cocktail stick inside for baking.

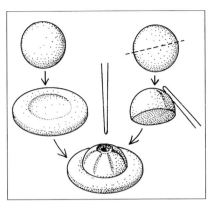

5 Form a 13mm (½in) ball of bronze clay and press it onto the board to make a disc 25mm (1in) across. Indent the centre with the large former. Form another 13mm (½in) ball and cut it in half. Press one half onto the disc. Flatten the top with the small former and indent a pattern round the side. Make a 3mm (⅛in) hole through the centre.

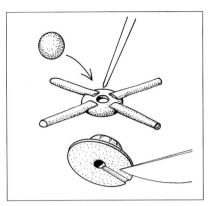

6 To make the shade holder, form a 6mm (¼in) ball of bronze clay and flatten onto the board into a disc 13mm (½in) across. Make a 3mm (⅛in) hole in the centre. Cut four 20mm (¾in) lengths from a log 3mm (⅛in) thick and press them onto the disc in a cross. Bake all the lamp base pieces for 30 minutes. Remove the cocktail stick while the clay is still warm. Cut a groove in the lamp base for the wire.

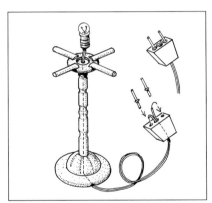

7 Trim the ends of the upright and glue to the base disc, ensuring that the holes align. Trim the shade holder so that it fits just inside the shade and glue it to the top of the upright. Remove the plug from the bulb wire and thread the wire down through the lamp base until the bulb sits on the top of the shade holder. Refit the plug and test the light. Glue the wire into the groove in the base.

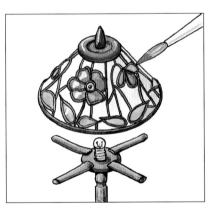

8 Paint the shade with the glass paints – red and yellow for the poppies, green for the leaves. Varnish the white parts with gloss varnish. Finally, fit the shade onto the shade holder; you can use a dab of glue, but you will need to be able to remove it to replace the bulb. Varnish the bronze parts of the lamp with matt varnish.

CHAPTER 5

DINING ROOM MINIATURES

A full roast dinner with all the trimmings is laid out in the dining room, and everything on the tables, apart from the glassware, is made with polymer clay. On the sideboard, luscious fruits and desserts stand waiting.

Instructions for most of the polymer clay miniatures in the photograph are to be found in this chapter. The remainder are given in projects on the following pages: pictures (page 102); flowers (page 94-97); vases (page 98); candlesticks (page 52); clock (page 50); bowl (page 24).

DINNER SERVICE

This white and gold dinner service will harmonize with virtually any doll's house colour scheme. The scalloped edges of the plates and vegetable dish covers disguise any irregularities in hand-made vessels, while the simple painted sprig design can be replaced by a more elaborate one if you wish.

MATERIALS

- Polymer clay: white
- Talcum powder
- 13mm (½in), 10mm (⅜in) and 6mm (¼in) formers (see page 24)
- 22mm (⅞in) marble
- Sandpaper
- Superglue
- Fine artist's paintbrush, size 00 or smaller
- Acrylic paint: gold
- Gloss varnish

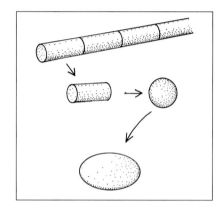

1 To make the dinner plates, form a log, 6mm (¼in) thick, of white clay and cut six 20mm (⅜in) lengths. Form one piece into a ball and press it down onto the board with the flat pad of your forefinger. Try to keep it as round as possible and work round the edge, thinning it until the centre is domed and the edge about 1mm (¹⁄₃₂in) thick. The plate should be about 22mm (⅞in) across.

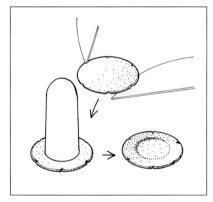

2 Using the back of a knife tip, make six indentations evenly spaced round the plate. Slice the plate off the board gently. Smear it with talc on both sides, and place it, right side up, on the board. Press the 13mm (½in) former into the centre to indent the plate and cause the edges to lift slightly. Repeat with the other clay pieces to make a set of plates. Bake for 10 minutes.

Small side plates are made in the same way.

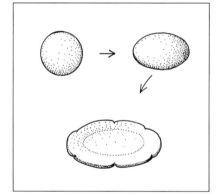

3 For the oval meat platter, form a 15mm (⅝in) ball of white clay, shape it into an oval and press down onto the board as for the plates, but keeping the oval shape. It should be about 35mm (1⅜in) long by 25mm (1in) wide. Indent the edges in the same way as the plates, slice off the board and use the 13mm (½in) former to make an oval impression in the centre. Bake for 10 minutes.

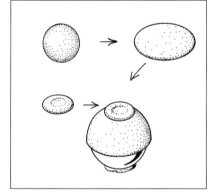

4 To make a vegetable dish, cut a 25mm (1in) length from a 6mm (¼in) thick log and form it into a ball. Follow the instructions on page 24 for making a bowl, using the marble. For the bowl base, flatten a 6mm (¼in) ball onto the board until it is 10mm (⅜in) across and indent the centre with a 6mm (¼in) former. Slice off the board and pat onto the centre of the bowl. Press the up-ended bowl, still on the marble, onto the board to flatten the base.

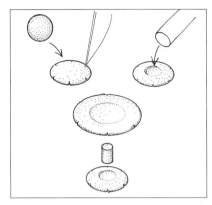

5 Make the lid in the same way as the plates but indent it with the 10mm (⅜in) former. The underside then becomes the top of the lid. Bake the bowl on the marble together with the lid for 10 minutes. Ease the bowl off the marble. Hold it inverted on a piece of sandpaper and rub with a circular motion to smooth the rim. Form a log, 1.5mm (¹⁄₁₆in) thick, of clay and flatten it slightly. Cut 10mm (⅜in) lengths and apply them to the sides of the bowl and the top of the lid for the handles.

6 To make the gravy boat, form an 8mm (⁵⁄₁₆in) ball of clay and mould it into a bowl shape by pushing it onto the rounded end of the small former, which has been dusted with talc. Remove from the former and pull into an oval shape. Apply a small disc for a foot and pull out a lip. See page 88 for instructions on applying a handle.

7 For the cake stand, make a large plate as in steps 1 and 2. Form a 6mm (¼in) ball and press onto the board as for the plates to make a 13mm (½in) disc as a base. Mark indentations all round as for the plates and press the centre with a 6mm (¼in) former. Form a log for the stem, 3mm (⅛in) thick and 13mm (½in) long. Bake the pieces for 10 minutes. Cut a 6mm (¼in) length from the log, keeping the cuts as straight as possible, and glue to the base and the plate.

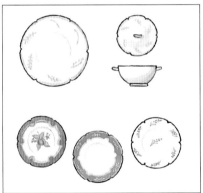

8 Coat all the china with gloss varnish. Paint the design with gold paint. (See page 25 for tips on painting miniature china.) Coat the china with another layer of gloss varnish. Alternative designs are shown in the illustration. If you are filling the gravy boat with gravy (see page 70), paint the design afterwards.

CUTLERY

Try to keep your hands cool when you are making miniature knives, forks and spoons in polymer clay. Once the pieces are formed, avoid handling them as much as possible. The knives are made by forming a block of clay into a blade-shaped cross-section, baking, and then cutting slices for the knife blades.

MATERIALS

- Polymer clay: navy blue, transparent, yellow
- Talcum powder
- Smooth round pencil
- Superglue
- Acrylic paint: silver

MIXTURES

- Bone = 4 transparent + 1 yellow

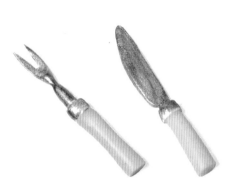

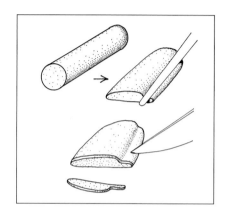

1 For the knives, form a log, 6mm (¼in) thick, of navy clay and flatten it onto the board until it is about 10mm (⅜in) wide. Indent one side with the side of a wool needle. Cut a slice from the end and see if it gives a good blade shape, adjusting the cross-section as necessary. Bake for 20 minutes. Now cut slices, 1mm (¹⁄₃₂in) thick, with a sharp knife blade.

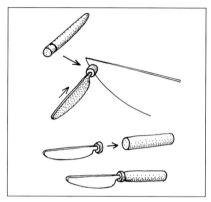

2 Form a log, 1.5mm (¹⁄₁₆in) thick, of navy clay and cut 1.5mm (¹⁄₁₆in) slices, applying one with your knife to the haft of each blade, pressing the haft right in. Form a log, 3mm (⅛in) thick, of bone clay for the handles. Bake the handles and blades for 10 minutes. (The blades will remain slightly flexible.) Cut six equal 10mm (⅜in) lengths from the handle log. Glue the blades to the handles.

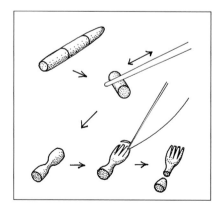

3 To make the forks, form a log of navy clay, a little less than 3mm (⅛in) thick. Cut lengths of 5mm (³⁄₁₆in). Groove the centre of each with a wool needle to thin it. Dust one end with talc and flatten it onto the board. Trim the end and make three cuts for the tines of the fork. Bake the forks for 10 minutes. Trim the handle end and then proceed as for step 2 to make the handles.

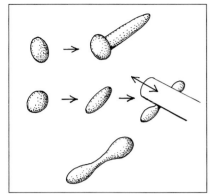

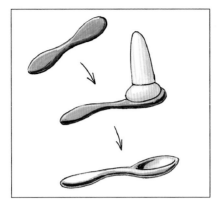

NAPKIN RINGS

These are simply thin strips of clay, marked along the edges and wrapped round a knitting needle, butting the ends together. Brush with silver powder, bake and then varnish. Use a small roll of white tissue or fabric for the napkin.

4 For the spoons, first make a spoon former. Form a 5mm (³⁄₁₆in) ball of clay and shape it into a slight oval. Form a handle from a short log of clay. Bake both oval and handle for 20 minutes and then glue the oval to the handle. Form a log, 3mm (⅛in) thick, and cut six 3mm (⅛in) lengths. Roll each into a ball and then into a short log 1.5mm (¹⁄₁₆in) thick. Use the pencil to thin the middle as for the forks, leaving a thin central section and a bulb at each end.

5 Flatten both the bulb ends slightly onto the board, slice off the board, turn over and place one on the pad of the talc-dusted finger of your left hand (right hand if you are left-handed). Stroke a little talc onto the clay and press the surface firmly with the spoon former. This will cup the spoon bowl and curve the handle slightly. Bake the spoons for 10 minutes.

Paint the spoons, the knife blades and the forks silver.

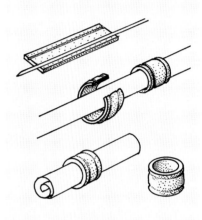

CRUET SET

Cruet sets of silver and glass first appeared in the late seventeenth century and are still popular today. This miniature set uses glass beads and metallic powder to simulate the crystal and silver.

MATERIALS

- Polymer clay: white
- 20mm (¾in) saucepan former (see page 28)
- Foil
- Knitting needle
- Silver-plated jump ring
- Metallic powder: silver
- Gloss varnish
- Superglue
- 4 round, cut glass or crystal beads, 8mm (⁵⁄₁₆in) in diameter
- Small glass bead, 3mm (⅛in) in diameter

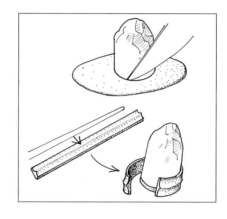

1 Cover the former with foil and smooth it down. Roll out a sheet of clay, 1.5mm (¹⁄₁₆in) thick, place the cut edge of the former onto it and cut round to cover the base. Cut a strip of clay from the sheet, 5mm (³⁄₁₆in) wide and about 7.5cm (3in) long, using a ruler to keep it straight. Indent the strip with two lines, using the side of a knitting needle. Now wrap the strip round the base of the former, cutting the ends to meet neatly.

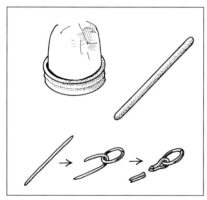

2 Form a log of clay, 1.5mm (¹⁄₁₆in) thick and 25mm (1in) long, for the central handle. (The ends will be trimmed after baking.) Form a log 1mm (¹⁄₃₂in) thick and thread it through the jump ring. Press the ends together and trim. Brush all the clay with silver powder and bake for 10 minutes. When cool, remove the former and varnish the silver powder.

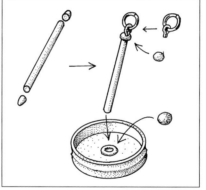

3 Trim the handle to 15mm (⅝in) long. Flatten a small ball of clay into the centre of the stand and indent this with the end of the handle. Press a small ball onto the top of the rod and push the loop of the jump ring onto this. Bake the pieces again and when cool, glue the central rod into the impression in the disc, taking care that it sets upright. Mix silver powder into a little varnish and paint the remaining white parts.

4 Form two 5mm (³⁄₁₆in) balls of clay and cut them in half for the tops of the bottles. Press one onto the top of three of the large beads. Mark a rim round each, and pierce the salt and pepper ones with holes. Press a small clay ball onto the top of the fourth bead and push the small bead onto this for the vinegar bottle. Brush the clay with silver powder, bake and varnish when cool. Arrange the bottles in the cruet stand.

PROFITEROLES

Choux pastry is thought to have first appeared in the mid-sixteenth century in France, and profiteroles, little choux buns drenched in chocolate or caramel sauce, are still universally popular.

MATERIALS

- Polymer clay: white, ochre, yellow
- Foil
- Artist's pastel: brown
- Acrylic paint: dark brown
- Gloss varnish
- Cake stand (see page 65)
- Superglue

MIXTURES

- Choux buns
  = 1 white + 1 ochre + 1 yellow

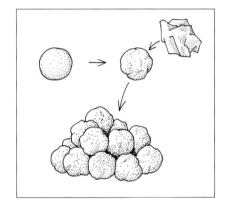

1 Form the choux bun mixture into small balls, about 5mm (³⁄₁₆in) in diameter, and press them all over with a piece of crumpled foil to texture the surface. Arrange them into a pyramid and brush with brown pastel. Bake for 10 minutes.

2 Glue the pyramid onto the cake stand and paint the profiteroles with brown acrylic paint to simulate a chocolate sauce drizzled over them. When the paint is dry, varnish the paint to give it a wet shine.

VARIATIONS

These instructions can be adapted to make chocolate cream eclairs. Form the choux buns mixture into ovals instead of balls and texture the surface. Cut a slit along each eclair and insert a log of white clay. Bake and then paint with brown paint for chocolate icing.

Further ideas are to use light brown paint for caramel eclairs or pink for a strawberry icing.

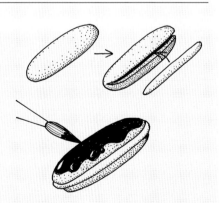

ROAST LAMB DINNER

Roast leg of lamb with roast potatoes, green beans and sliced carrots make up the menu for the first course of this polymer clay feast. Food is fun to make with polymer clay and easy enough for most levels of ability.

MATERIALS
- Polymer clay: white, ochre, beige, orange, leaf green, light brown, red, transparent, yellow
- Foil
- Artist's pastel: burnt sienna, golden-yellow, dark brown, black, crimson
- Gloss varnish

MIXTURES
- Bone = 4 transparent + 2 white + 1 ochre;
- Pink = 8 white + 1 scant red;
- Meat = marble lightly 1 pink + 2 light brown;
- Fat = 1 ochre + 8 transparent

1 Form several 5mm (³⁄₁₆in) balls of beige clay for the potatoes, shape them into ovals and cut them in halves and quarters. Rub some yellow and brown artist's pastel onto paper and roll the potato pieces around on the paper, brushing the loose powder over them to give them a 'browned' effect. Bake for 10 minutes and varnish with gloss varnish when cool, to suggest an oily shine.

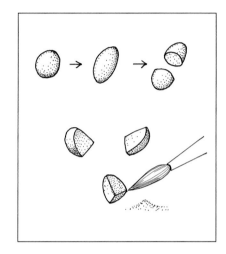

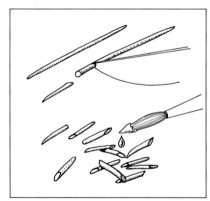

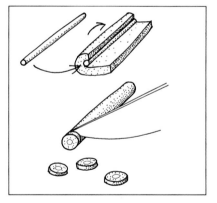

2 For the green beans, form several logs, 1mm (¹⁄₃₂in) thick, of leaf green, each about 5cm (2in) long. Cut into rough 5mm (³⁄₁₆in) lengths and bake for 10 minutes. They do not have to be separated for baking as they can be pulled apart easily afterwards. Varnish with gloss varnish to give them a wet look. This is most easily done by making a small cup of foil and stirring the beans up with some varnish.

3 To make the sliced carrots, mix a little white with orange to lighten it. Form a log, 1.5mm (¹⁄₁₆in) thick, of the light orange mixture. Roll flat a small sheet of orange clay, about 3mm (¹⁄₈in) thick, and roll the light orange up in it. Thin by rolling on the board until it is 3mm (¹⁄₈in) thick. Bake for 10 minutes and, before it cools, cut 1mm (¹⁄₃₂in) thick slices. Varnish as for the beans.

4 Make the gravy by mixing water-based gloss varnish with brown acrylic paint. Press an oval of dark brown clay into the bottom of the gravy boat and bake for 10 minutes. Now put a thick layer of the varnish gravy on top.

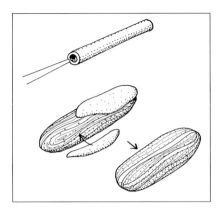

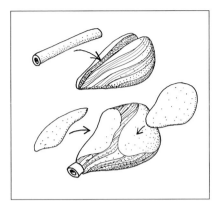

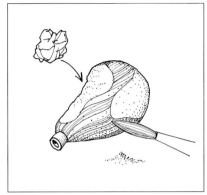

5 For the meat, first make the bone by forming a log, 3mm (⅛in) thick, of bone-coloured clay, 25mm (1in) long, and poking a deep hole in one end. Bake for 10 minutes and trim the end with the hole to make it look cut. Roll flat some fat mixture clay and apply round a log of the marbled meat mixture. Fold and roll a few times so that the transparent clay makes streaks of fat in the meat.

6 Form the meat into a 20mm (¾in) ball and shape it into a joint, keeping the streaks running lengthways. Cut a slit halfway into the joint, insert the bone with the end protruding and squeeze them back together. Apply some thin sheets of fat to the outside.

7 Crumple a small piece of foil and use this to apply a crinkly texture all over the meat. Rub the yellow, black and brown pastels onto a piece of paper and brush the powder all over the meat. Texture again with the foil if necessary. Bake for 10 minutes.

8 While it is still hot, quickly brush gloss varnish all over the meat and then cut a few slices. Brush a little crimson pastel powder onto the centre of the cut pieces and varnish again. To assemble a complete plate, place slices of meat with vegetables on the plate and dribble over some of the varnish gravy.

BLANCMANGES

Blancmanges were popular from Regency times right through to Edwardian banquets. The blancmanges are served on plates that have been stamped and then brushed with silver powder.

MATERIALS

- Polymer clay: white, transparent, crimson, yellow
- 20mm (¾in) and 13mm (½in) formers (see page 28)
- Talcum powder
- Small charm (see page 16)
- Gloss varnish
- Serving plates
- Superglue

MIXTURES

- Pink blancmange
  = transparent + trace of crimson;
- Yellow blancmange
  = 8 transparent + 1 yellow;
- Strawberry blancmange = 1 yellow + 1 crimson

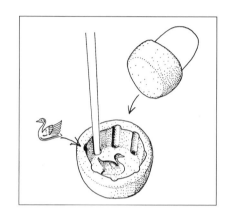

1 To make the mould, form a ball of white clay about 25mm (1in) in diameter. Press this onto the larger former, pushing the clay up the sides until you have a simple pot shape. Press the mould down onto the board and remove the former. Brush some talcum powder into the mould and press a small charm onto the bottom to make an impression. Remove the charm by lifting an edge with a needle and tipping it out. Use the handle of a paintbrush to make indentations all round the sides of the mould. Bake the mould for 20 minutes.

2 Dust the mould with talc and form a smooth ball of pink blancmange mixture, slightly larger than the inside of the mould. Shape the ball into an oval and press it into the mould, pushing it down firmly. Ease the clay away from the sides and gently pull the moulded clay out. Use blunt tools to emphasize the form. Bake for 10 minutes and, while it is warm, cut the rough base off to give a flat bottom. Varnish with gloss varnish.

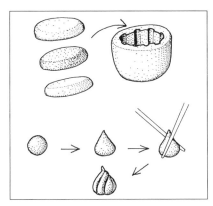

3 The layered blancmange is made by pressing flattened discs of different coloured clay into the mould and proceeding as above. The lemon blancmange is made using a smaller mould with a different charm as a motif. Place the blancmanges onto the plates. Form small balls of white into tear drops and press them lightly onto the board. Use two needles to mark them into rosettes.

4 The strawberries are small balls of clay, formed into ovals and marked all over with a pin in little lines. Make dents in the centre of the rosettes with the handle of a paintbrush and press on the strawberries. Place the decorations onto the plates around the blancmanges. Bake again for 10 minutes (this will not harm the varnish). Varnish the strawberries.

FRUIT STAND WITH FRUIT

Apples, oranges and black grapes are displayed in a silver fruit stand.
Fruit is fun to make in polymer clay – if the apples are a little irregular,
it adds to the realism, and a bunch of grapes can be any shape you like!
As with all food, colour is very important.

MATERIALS

- Polymer clay: white, yellow, green, orange, dark brown, crimson, blue, leaf green
- 25mm (1in) marble
- Small stamp (see pages 19-20)
- Silver metallic powder
- Gloss varnish
- Superglue
- Artist's pastel: crimson
- Wire suede brush or toothbrush
- Talcum powder
- Wax polish

MIXTURES

- Apple
  = 1 white + 1 yellow + trace of green;
- Grape = 1 blue + 1 crimson;
- Grape leaf = 1 leaf green + 1 yellow

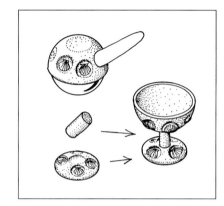

1 For the fruit stand, make a bowl using white clay and the marble as on page 24. Flatten the bowl bottom by pressing it onto the board and stamp a pattern around the bowl. Make a base as for the cake stand on page 65 and stamp it at regular intervals. Brush all the pieces with silver powder and bake for 10 minutes. Varnish and assemble as for the cake stand. Paint the inside of the bowl silver.

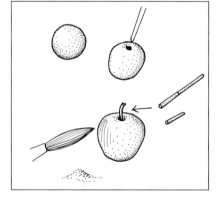

2 Form the apple mixture into 6mm (¼in) balls, varying the size a little. Make holes in the top and bottom of each ball with a wool needle and brush with crimson pastel, using a stiff brush so that it makes streaks down the apple sides. Cut a tiny stalk of dark brown clay and insert into the top hole of each apple.

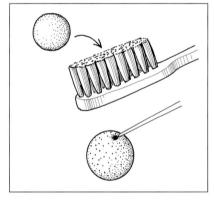

3 For the oranges, form 6mm (¼in) balls of orange clay and roll them lightly on the surface of a wire brush or toothbrush to texture the skin. Make slight holes in the top and bottom with a wool needle.

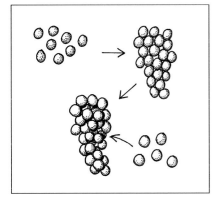

THE FLOWER ARRANGEMENT

Delicate roses, carnations and freesias fill a 'silver' basket as the table centrepiece. The instructions for making the flowers are in Chapter 7, and those for the basket are on page 36. Paint the basket silver and push a piece of air-drying clay into the bottom of the basket into which the flowers can be inserted.

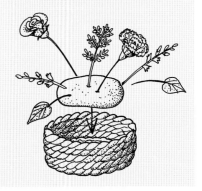

4 Make lots of 1.5mm (⅟₁₆in) balls of the grape mixture and lay them on the board in the shape of a bunch, pressing them together lightly. When the bunch is large enough, about 20mm (¾in) long, add grapes in a second layer to plump out the middle. Finally, lift the bunch off the board and add grapes to the back of the bunch in the same way.

5 Poke a thin stalk of grape leaf green into the top of the bunch. Roll out the same green and cut a leaf shape, marking veins. Pat this onto the top of the bunch and trail a few fine tendrils downwards. Brush the leaf with a little crimson pastel and the grapes with talc to represent a bloom. Bake all the fruit for 10 minutes. Rub a little wax polish on the apples to make them shine and arrange the fruit in the fruit stand.

CHAPTER 6

TEATIME IN THE CONSERVATORY

Tea for two with a dainty tea set and delectable cakes is laid in the Victorian conservatory, which holds a profusion of plants. Polymer clay can be used to make very effective pot plants – the fine texture of the clay means that leaves can be made extremely thin and realistic, while the transparent clay gives flowers a delicate translucency. The plant pots are made using the potting technique in a variety of clay colours, including terracotta and stone-effect clays.

All the polymer clay miniatures in the photograph are projects in this chapter apart from the plates, which are found on page 64.

GERANIUMS

Cheerful geraniums are not difficult to make in miniature and are attractive on doll's house window-sills. Coffee grounds make realistic soil, but in smaller pots, simple texturing of the 'soil' surface with a needle is an alternative.

MATERIALS

- Polymer clay: light brown, red, white, green, leaf green, dark brown, crimson, transparent
- Florist's fine green wire, no. 32
- Fine-nosed pliers
- Superglue
- PVA glue (optional)
- Coffee grounds (optional)

MIXTURES

- Terracotta
  = 2 light brown + 1 red + 1 white;
- Geranium leaf green
  = 1 green + 1 yellow + 2 leaf green;
- Geranium leaf centre
  = 2 geranium leaf green + 1 crimson;
- Geranium pink
  = transparent + trace of crimson

VARIATIONS

Try making the geranium flowers in a variety of colours. The leaves can also have variations of green – try pale green centres or variegated greens. The hydrangeas in the photograph are made in the same way, using blue clay or transparent clay brushed with blue, mauve and green artist's pastel. The leaves are made as for the trailing plant leaves on page 84, notched at the base, and glued in pairs up the stems. Try using the back of a real leaf to impress the veins on the clay.

1 To make the pots, form a ball of terracotta clay 20mm (¾in) in diameter and roll it into an egg shape. Cut it in half to make two pots. Flatten the bottom of one on the board and roll it on its side to straighten the sides, keeping it cone-shaped. Now follow the instructions for potting larger vessels on page 25, using, first, a wool needle and then a paintbrush handle as the sides thin.

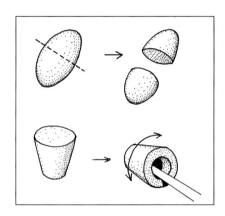

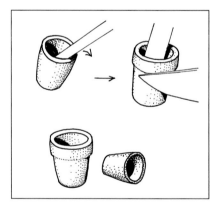

2 Periodically up-end the pot on the board and press down to flatten the rim and bottom. Finally, flare out the top of the pot a little by pressing outwards with a paintbrush handle while you turn the pot in your hands. Mark a rim by pressing the side of the knife against the pot all round. Make several pots in different sizes and bake for 10 minutes.

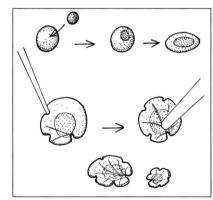

3 For the geranium leaves, form 3mm (⅛in) balls of geranium leaf green and 1.5mm (¹⁄₁₆in) balls of the leaf centre green. Press a small ball onto a larger ball and flatten onto the board until it is about 8mm (⁵⁄₁₆in) across. Make indentations all round the edge and a deeper one at the base for the stalk. Mark veins. Slice off the board and indent the centre a little. Make at least five leaves for each plant, some smaller than the others.

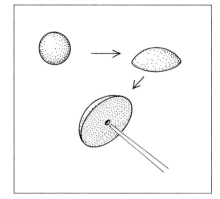

4 To make the geranium flowers, form a 6mm (¼in) ball of geranium pink clay and press it onto the board, leaving it domed. Slice off the board and make a hole in the underside with a wool needle for the stalk. Press lightly back onto the board.

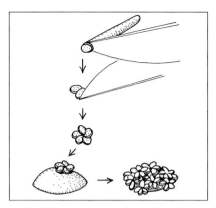

5 Form a log, 1.5mm (¹⁄₁₆in) thick, of pink clay. Cut a thin slice as a petal, lift it on the tip of the knife and press it down onto the board. Cut another petal, place this just overlapping the first and continue round until you have a five-petal flower. Slice the flower off the board and lift onto the dome with your knife. Make more flowers, patting them lightly onto the dome until it is covered, with some overhanging the edge. Make a hole in the centre of each flower.

6 Half fill one of the pots with scrap clay. Form a ball of dark brown, flatten it and press it onto the scrap clay, covering it completely. Texture the surface if you are not going to use coffee grounds for soil. Make about five deep holes in the clay with a wool needle for the stalks.

7 Bake the ger... ...s and the pots. Cut some 25mm (1in) lengths of green wire and glue them to the backs of the leaves, gluing some as two leaves on a single stalk. Glue the end of a stalk into the hole underneath the flower head. Glue the leaves and flower into the pot, making sure that the larger leaves are lower than the small ones. If you are using coffee grounds, flood the top of the 'soil' with PVA glue and sprinkle on the grounds. Tip off the excess when the glue is dry.

VARIATIONS

You can make a pretty trailing geranium by applying geranium leaves to wired stems from the project on page 84. Make geranium flowers and insert them into the top of the pot.

FERNS

Ferns were a great favourite in Victorian conservatories and parlours. The polymer clay leaves are cut into feathery shapes and draped over foil while they are baking to give them a natural curve.

MATERIALS
- Polymer clay: granite, dark brown, leaf green, yellow, white
- Paper clip
- Pin
- Foil
- Florist's fine green wire, no. 32
- Superglue
- PVA glue
- Coffee grounds

MIXTURES
- Fern green = 1 yellow + 1 leaf green;
- Light green = 2 fern green + 1 white

VARIATIONS

An aspidistra can be made in exactly the same way, but use leaf green clay and instead of cutting the leaves into fronds, press a real long-veined leaf onto them to make veins. Varnish with matt varnish for a slight gloss. The palm is made by applying long, thin slices of clay to the board in a fan shape, then slicing them off the board and baking them, curved over foil. Glue wire to the back of the palms and arrange in a pot.

1 For the 'granite' urn, form a 20mm (¾in) ball of granite clay and follow the instructions for potting larger vessels on page 25. Decorate the sides with impressions made with a paper clip and mark a deep rim. Bake for 10 minutes. Half fill the pot with scrap clay and then press a disc of dark brown on top, large enough to cover the scrap clay. Make at least nine holes in the 'soil'.

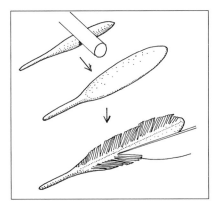

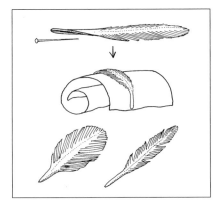

2 Form five 10mm (⅜in) balls of fern green clay and roll them into tapered logs, 5cm (2in) long and 5mm (³⁄₁₆in) thick at the widest point, tapering to 1.5mm (¹⁄₁₆in) for the stalk. Roll flat the thick part until it is about 13mm (½in) wide at the widest point and less than 1mm (¹⁄₃₂in) thick. Leave the stem unflattened. Mark a central line and make cuts at an angle all down each side of the leaf. Flick up some of the fronds with your knife.

3 Lift the stalk and press down onto a pin to indent the back for the wire. Carefully slice under the leaf to free it from the board and lift it onto a curved piece of foil. Make four more leaves.

Make two leaves more circular in shape for the bottom leaves. Use the light green to make two smaller leaves for the centre of the plant. Lay all the leaves over the foil and bake for 15 minutes with the soil-filled pot.

4 Cut nine pieces of wire, each 13mm (½in) long. Glue a wire into the back of each stalk. Poke the stalks into the holes in the clay soil, arranging the leaves so that the rounded ones are to the outside and the smaller ones in the centre. Apply PVA glue and coffee grounds as for the geraniums on page 79.

LILIES

*Lilies come in a wide range of colours, and the flowers are useful
in arrangements – both full size and miniature! Try making lilies with white
flowers and pink stamens or orange flowers with yellow stamens.*

MATERIALS

- Polymer clay: golden-yellow, orange, transparent, leaf green, dark brown
- Talcum powder
- Baked pot, 15mm (⅝in) in diameter, made with white clay (see page 78)
- Florist's fine green wire, no. 32
- Jam jar
- Superglue
- Coffee grounds
- PVA glue

MIXTURES

- Mix a little of the yellow and orange clays into transparent to make them more translucent.

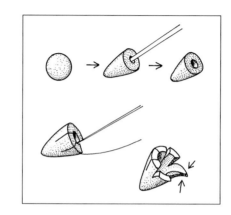

1 To make the flowers, form a 5mm (³⁄₁₆in) ball of yellow clay and shape it into a cone. Make a hole in the centre with a wool needle. Twist the needle inside the hole to splay out the sides. Place the little trumpet on the board and make six cuts all round. Hold the base of the flower in one hand and, with the other, pull out each of the sections in turn, pinching them into points.

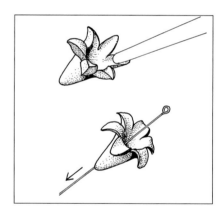

2 Dust your fingers with talc and press each petal against your finger with a paintbrush handle to thin and cup it. Cut a 25mm (1in) length of wire, turn a tiny loop in the end and thread the wire through the centre of the flower, pulling the loop into the clay (see page 29). Bend back the petals slightly.

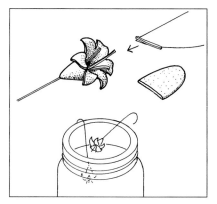

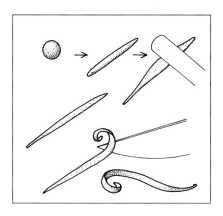

4 For the leaves, form a 3mm (⅛in) ball of leaf green, and shape it into a log about 30mm (1¼in) long and pointed at each end. Roll one end flat and slice it off the board, which will cause it to curl. Straighten slightly and lay it carefully on its side on the baking sheet so that it retains the curve. Make about four more leaves, varying the size a little.

3 Form a log of orange, 3mm (⅛in) thick, and roll it flat. Cut tiny slices for stamens. Lift each on the tip of your knife and press into the centre of the flower. Bend a loop in the end of the wire and hang the flowers inside a jam jar to bake. Make two more flowers and a bud, which is simply an oval of clay on a wire.

5 Half fill the white pot with scraps of clay and press a disc of dark brown on top. Make about ten deep holes in the clay soil with a wool needle. Bake all the pieces for about 10 minutes. Bend the flower heads at right angles and arrange with the leaves in the pot. Apply glue and coffee grounds as for the geraniums on page 79.

TRAILING PLANT

*This project uses marbled clay to give the variegated leaf of a devil's ivy (Scindapsus).
To make a philodendron, use plain dark green clay. The leaves are simply pressed onto
clay-covered wires, which can be bent into shape after baking.*

MATERIALS

- ◆ Polymer clay: leaf green, white, yellow, dark brown
- ◆ Fine beading wire
- ◆ Baked pot, 25mm (1in) in diameter, made with granite clay (see page 78; in this project, the pot has been stamped to resemble carved stone)
- ◆ Sandpaper
- ◆ Superglue

MIXTURES

- ◆ Marble together leaf green and white for a variegated green;
- ◆ Mix a trace of yellow into the marbled clay for the young leaves

VARIATIONS

To make a hanging plant, pierce holes in the rim of a pot or bowl before baking and then attach fine cords. Polymer clay baskets also make pretty hanging containers.

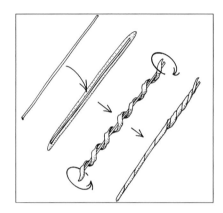

1 Form five or six long thin stems of leaf green clay, 1mm (¹⁄₃₂in) thick and varying in length from 25mm (1in) to 50mm (2in). Flatten each onto the board. Cut pieces of beading wire, the same lengths, and press one onto the centre of each stem. Slice off the board and then twist the clay stem round the wire so it forms a spiral. Roll very lightly on the board so that the spiral forms a continuous covering of clay.

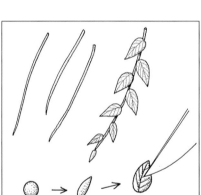

2 Make plenty of 3mm (⅛in) balls from the marbled clay, point one end of each and flatten onto the board for the leaves. Mark on veins, slice off the board and press the base of each leaf firmly onto the stem. Form a few smaller leaves of the young leaf mixture and apply these to the tips. Slice under each stem with the knife and transfer to the baking sheet. Make a few extra large leaves.

3 Prepare the pot with 'soil' as on page 83. Bake with the stems and leaves for 10 minutes. Glue the stems into the holes in the pot soil, arranging them round the pot to trail outwards and bending them into a natural curve. Glue the spare leaves onto the top of the pot. If some stems are too long, trim them and glue the tips into the soil to make the plant bushier.

FRUIT CAKE

Cakes are enjoyable miniatures to make with polymer clay – the various textures are easily simulated to make delicious-looking treats. The instructions given here and in the next project can be used as a basis for dozens of different cakes by varying the colours and decorations.

MATERIALS
♦ Polymer clay: ochre, light brown
♦ Mix Quick mixing medium (see page 26)
♦ Sand
♦ Black poppy seeds
♦ Small bowl
♦ Artist's pastel: burnt sienna

MIXTURES
♦ Cake brown = 1 ochre + 1 light brown

VARIATIONS

The scones in the photograph are made in exactly the same way but use the sponge cake mixture clay on page 86. Indent the sides with the side of a needle all round and brush with brown pastel powder. When they are cool, split and apply a few slices of a yellow and transparent mix for the butter. Bake again and varnish the butter.

1 Form a 15mm (⅝in) ball of the cake brown clay and mix in a 10mm (⅜in) ball of Mix Quick to soften it. Pour some sand and some poppy seeds into a bowl and press the clay onto them. Work the sand and seeds into the clay by folding and rolling, dipping it into the mixture to add more until it is evenly mixed through. Cut the clay in half to check – it needs to look like a well-fruited loaf.

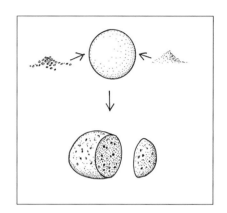

2 Shape the clay into a ball and flatten it slightly. Roll it on its side to make a cake shape. Indent just inside the edge around the top with a paintbrush handle to make it look like a risen cake. Rub the pastel on paper to release the powder and brush the surface liberally with this. Bake for 10 minutes and when cool, cut a slice or two.

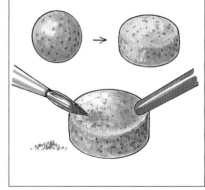

Sponge Sandwich Cakes

Delicious lemon and chocolate cakes adorn the tea table. Translucent clay with a touch of added colour makes simple cake icing, which looks very like real glacé icing and is easy to apply.

MATERIALS

Chocolate Cake
- Polymer clay: light brown, dark brown, ochre, white
- Mix Quick mixing medium (see page 26)
- 1 teaspoon ground nutmeg
- Small bowl
- Matt and gloss varnish

Lemon Cake
- Polymer clay: white, ochre, yellow, transparent, orange
- Mix Quick mixing medium (see page 26)
- 1 teaspoon semolina
- Small bowl
- Artist's pastel: burnt sienna

MIXTURES

Chocolate Cake
- Textured chocolate cake mix = 15mm (⅝in) ball light brown clay + 10mm (⅜in) ball Mix Quick + approximately 1 teaspoon ground nutmeg;
- Chocolate icing = 13mm (½in) ball dark brown + 6mm (¼in) ball Mix Quick;
- Walnut = 2 ochre + 1 white

Lemon Cake
- Sponge cake colour
  = 1 white + 1 yellow + 1 ochre;
- Textured sponge mix = 15mm (⅝in) ball sponge cake colour clay + 10mm (⅜in) ball Mix Quick + approximately 1 teaspoon semolina;
- Lemon icing
  = 1 yellow + 4 transparent;
- Orange slice
  = 1 orange + 2 transparent

1 To make the chocolate cake, follow step 1 of the fruit cake instructions on page 85, working the nutmeg and Mix Quick into the clay. Form two 13mm (½in) balls of this textured chocolate cake mixture and flatten on the board to make two 20mm (¾in) cakes. Form an 8mm (⁵⁄₁₆in) ball of dark brown clay and squeeze it in your fingers into a 20mm (¾in) disc for the filling. Assemble the cakes with the filling in the middle. Roll the cake lightly on its side on the board. Bake the cake for 5 minutes.

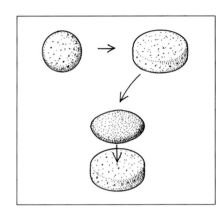

2 Form a 13mm (½in) ball of the chocolate icing mixture, shape it into a disc and press onto the top of the still-warm cake. Work the icing down the sides and stroke the icing all over with a finger tip to remove fingerprints. Form seven 1.5mm (¹⁄₁₆in) balls of walnut colour, shape them into ovals and press onto the board. Mark a line down the centre of each and indent the sides.

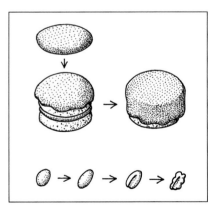

VARIATIONS

The iced fancies in the photograph are simply little blocks of icing decorated with cream rosettes and small pieces of coloured clay to suggest crystallized violets and cherries. The pink icing colour is made by mixing a trace of crimson into transparent clay. The white icing is transparent clay.

3 Decorate the cake with the walnuts. Cut a slice from the cake, through the baked and unbaked clay – cutting now gives the icing a soft look. Bake the cake for 10 minutes and varnish the chocolate icing with a mixture of matt and gloss varnish.

Make the lemon cake in exactly the same way with the textured sponge cake mixture. The centre looks good with a layer of white to suggest cream. Bake as for the chocolate cake and then apply the lemon icing. Make cream rosettes (see page 73).

4 To make the orange slices, form a log, 3mm (⅛in) thick, of orange slice mixture. Roll out a sheet of transparent clay to 1mm (1/32in) thick and wrap this around the orange. Roll the resulting cane on the board to thin it and press it into a triangular cross section. Cut into six equal lengths and assemble. Roll out a 1mm (1/32in) sheet of orange clay and use it to wrap the assembled lengths. Roll this on the board to thin it to about 3mm (⅛in) thick. Now use tiny slices to decorate the top of the cake, along with the cream rosettes. Cut a slice from the cake and bake for 10 minutes.

TEA SET

Polymer clay makes very realistic doll's house china because it can be made so thin. Various ideas for painting the tea set are given here, and you can use colours to match your doll's house rooms.

MATERIALS
- Polymer clay: white
- Thick wool needle
- 6mm (¼in) former (see page 24)
- Pen cap
- Small marble
- Talcum powder
- Sandpaper
- Acrylic paints: pink and soft green
- Fine artist's paintbrush, size 00 or smaller
- Gloss varnish

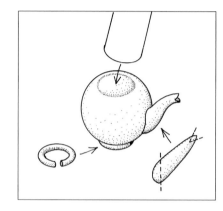

1 To make the teapot, form a 15mm (⅝in) ball of white clay. Roll a log 1.5mm (¹⁄₁₆in) thick and cut a 20mm (¾in) length. Form this into a ring and press the ball onto it to make the foot. Press the end of a pen cap onto the top of the ball. Form a 6mm (¼in) ball and shape it into a 20mm (¾in) long tapered log for the spout. Trim the thick end at an angle and cut a V-shape out of the thin end. Press onto the teapot and curve to shape.

2 Form a log, 1.5mm (¹⁄₁₆in) thick, and cut a 13mm (½in) length for the handle. Press on one end, with the handle lying upwards, and then curve the handle over and down and press it gently against the lower part of the teapot to secure. Roll a tiny ball and press it onto the top for the lid handle.

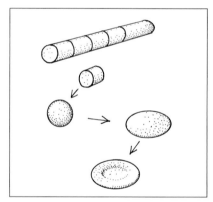

3 For the saucers, form a log 6mm (¼in) thick and cut six 6mm (¼in) lengths. Form these into balls. Follow the instructions on page 64 for the dinner plates, using the 6mm (¼in) former and omitting the indentations, to make saucers 15mm (⅝in) in diameter.

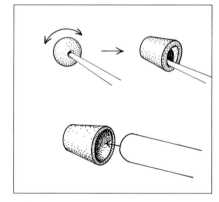

4 To make the cups, form a log 6mm (¼in) thick and cut six 6mm (¼in) lengths. Roll each into as round a ball as you can. Follow the technique for potting the clay on page 25. When the cup has formed and the sides are thinning, gently remove the needle and press the cup onto the rounded end of the 6mm (¼in) former, which has been dusted with talc.

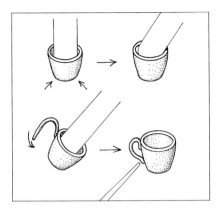

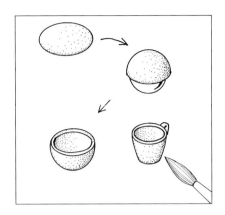

5 Gently press the bottom of the cup down onto the board to flatten it. At this point, you can pinch the cup bottom a little to shape it and flare out the lip by rotating the former inside. Make the cup handle in the same way as for the teapot but use a thinner log, 10mm (⅜in) long. Apply the handle while the cup is still on its former to prevent it distorting. Make more cups to match.

6 For the milk jug, form a 6mm (¼in) ball of white clay and pull out a small point at the top. Slice the end off this so that it is flat. Push the point of a wool needle into the top and rotate it, flaring out the clay evenly. Push the wool needle further down to give an illusion of depth when you look into the top of the jug. Pull out a spout with the tip of the needle. Apply a handle as for the cups, making sure it is exactly opposite the spout.

7 The sugar basin is a small version of the bowl on page 24 made on a small marble.

Bake all the crockery for 20 minutes. When cool, sand any irregularities. Varnish all the crockery with gloss varnish. Allow to dry thoroughly and then brush with nail varnish remover to remove any grease before painting.

8 Paint the tea set as shown in the illustration, following the instructions on painting china on page 25. Alternative designs are also given.

When the paint is completely dry, varnish again to protect the paint.

CHAPTER 7

BEDROOM
MINIATURES

T he doll's house bedroom provides an ideal opportunity
for making delicate and charming miniatures. Vases of
flowers, pretty picture frames and dressing table silverware
and beads all show the versatility of polymer clay in a
bedroom setting. The 'marquetry' sewing box is filled with
tiny sewing things and the bedside lamp is electrified.

The photograph shows the wide variety of miniatures
that can be made from the projects in this chapter with the
exception of the following, which are described elsewhere in
this book: bowl (page 24); jug (page 89); book (page 56); cup
and saucer (page 88); soap (page 115); stool (page 109).

DRESSING TABLE SET

Silver dressing table sets were an important accessory for the Victorian lady, and this miniature version mimics the embossed silver designs that were so popular. The instructions give two different methods of making miniature brushes, and the techniques can be adapted to make many other types of miniature brush, such as the kitchen brush and broom.

MATERIALS

- Polymer clay: black, various colours for beads
- Small stamps taken from charms and silverware (see page 20)
- Metallic powder: silver
- Small piece of fur fabric
- Piece of mirror-effect wrapping paper (patterned papers are often plain 'silver' on the back)
- Ceramic tile
- Cocktail stick cut into a 13mm (½in) length
- Gloss varnish
- Superglue
- Household paintbrush with soft bristles
- PVA glue
- Beading wire

ACCESSORIES

The glass bottles and jars are simply glass beads in a variety of shapes, colours and sizes. Make the lids by pressing on small balls of different coloured clays and then baking and varnishing them (see the instructions for the cruet bottles on page 68). Some of the lids have been dusted with gold or silver powder.
The comb is a flat strip of clay with the teeth marked in with a knife.

1 To make the hairbrush, form a 10mm (⅜in) ball of black clay, shape it into an oval and press it down onto the board until it is about 3mm (⅛in) thick and domed in the centre. Form an 8mm (⁵⁄₁₆in) ball of clay and shape it into a short log. Thin the centre and press down onto the board for the handle, pushing one end into a concave curve. Press this end against the oval.

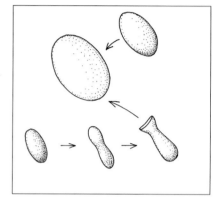

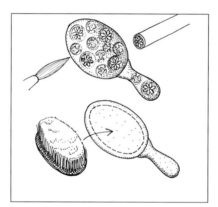

2 Impress the surface of the clay with the small stamps, taking care not to press too hard at the edges, or you will distort the clay. Brush all over with silver powder. Bake for 10 minutes and varnish when cool. Cut an oval-shaped piece of fur fabric to fit the head of the brush, allowing a narrow border all round. Glue into place.

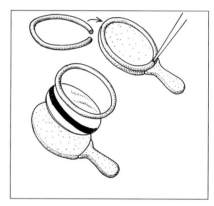

3 To make the hand mirror, follow the instructions for the brush handle. After baking and varnishing, press a thin log of clay round the edge of the oval area and smooth the edges. Brush with silver powder and bake again for 10 minutes. Carefully remove the applied rim, which should not have stuck fast as it was applied over the varnish. Varnish the rim. Glue an oval of mirror-effect wrapping paper to the mirror head and glue the rim back over it.

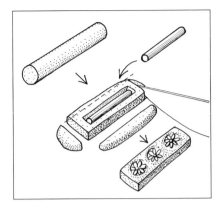

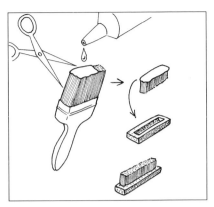

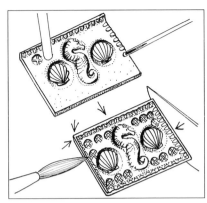

4 To make the clothes brush, form a log, 5mm (³/₁₆in) thick, of black, flatten it slightly and press the length of cocktail stick into the centre of the log. Trim all round the cocktail stick into a neat rectangle for the brush back. Turn it over and, with the cocktail stick still in place, stamp the back to match the other pieces. Brush with silver powder, bake for 10 minutes and remove the cocktail stick. Varnish over the silver powder.

5 Trim the end of the household paintbrush to square it and apply a thick layer of PVA glue on the end of the bristles. Allow the adhesive to dry. Cut a section of bristles away from the paintbrush to fit the groove made by the cocktail stick. Glue into place, using PVA glue, allow to dry and trim the bristles.

6 To make the tray, roll out a sheet of black clay on the tile to 1.5mm (¹/₁₆in) thick, and trim to 25 x 20mm (1 x ¾in). Use one or two small stamps to impress a pattern onto the centre. Mark the edge with the eye of a wool needle, which will scallop it. Cut under the edge 3mm (⅛in) all round with the knife and lift it up to make the sides of the tray, pinching the corners into shape. Brush the top with silver powder and bake on the tile for 20 minutes. Varnish when cool.

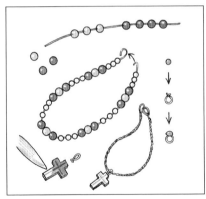

7 The jewellery scattered on the tray is made by threading tiny beads onto beading wire. You can make beads out of clay by piercing 1.5mm (¹/₁₆in) balls onto a length of fine wire and baking. Remove from the wire when they are still warm and re-thread, interspersing with tiny glass beads. The rings are tiny loops of wire with a 1.5mm (¹/₁₆in) ball of coloured clay pressed onto the join and baked. The pendants are made out of clay and brushed with metallic powder.

ROSES AND MAIDENHAIR FERN

Roses can be made in a glorious range of colours, from crimson through to delicate pastel shades. Artist's pastels can also be used to tip the petals with colour. The maidenhair fern is a delicate but useful filler for tiny floral arrangements.

MATERIALS

- Polymer clay: transparent, red, leaf green
- Fine florist's wire, no. 32, cut into 4cm (1½in) lengths with a small loop turned in the top of each (see page 29)
- Glue stick
- Talcum powder
- 10mm (⅜in) crockery former (see page 24)
- Jam jar
- Beading wire
- Air-drying clay
- Tweezers

MIXTURES

- Make three different shades of pink – dark, medium and light – by mixing tiny amounts of red into transparent clay

1 Wrap the loop of each wire in a tiny ball of dark pink clay and bake for 10 minutes to make the rose centres. Form a log, 3mm (⅛in) thick, of dark pink clay and cut three 1.5mm (¹⁄₁₆in) slices. Flatten each of these onto the board, brush with talc and then press each one firmly with the flat end of the former to make each into a round, paper-thin petal. Slice under each petal with the knife, to free it from the board.

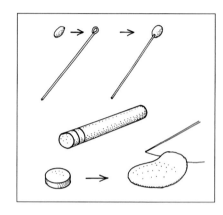

2 Smear a rose centre with the glue stick and apply the petal, squeezing it onto the baked clay. Apply the other two petals in the same way, curving them round the centre more loosely. Make two petals of medium pink clay and apply them in the same way, but keeping them more open and bending the tops outwards. Finally, make three petals of light pink clay and apply them loosely round the outside.

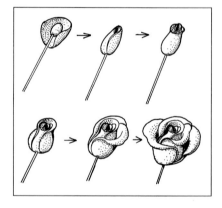

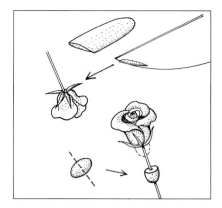

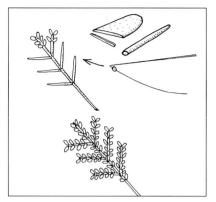

3 To make the sepals, roll flat some leaf green clay and cut tiny spikes with your knife. Hold the rose upside down and apply each sepal with your knife. Form a 3mm (⅛in) oval of leaf green and cut it in half. Thread this onto the stalk of the rose, pushing it up against the base.

Repeat for more roses, making some with fewer petals for buds. Bend a hook in the bottom of each stalk and hang them inside a jam jar to bake.

4 To make the maidenhair fern, insert a length of beading wire into a stem of leaf green clay, 1mm (½₂in) thick and 25mm (1in) long (see page 84). Flatten a log of leaf green and cut thin slices to apply to the stem for side stems. Now cut tiny slices from a log, 1.5mm (⅟₁₆in) thick, of leaf green and apply these with your knife tip to the side stems, overlapping them slightly for strength. Finally, slice the fern off the board and curve it slightly for baking. Bake the roses and ferns for 10 minutes.

5 Press a small ball of air-drying clay into the bottom of a vase. Arrange the flowers by inserting the ends of the stems into the clay. You will need to trim some stems to make the flowers different lengths for an attractive arrangement and to bend the wires into a natural curve. Use tweezers to hold the stalks as you insert each into the clay. Arrange the ferns below the roses and in the spaces between them.

CARNATIONS

This project makes snowy white carnations, but you can make them in a variety of colours. Try tipping the petals with acrylic paint in a contrasting colour after baking.

MATERIALS

- Polymer clay: white, transparent, leaf green
- Fine florist's wire, no. 32, cut into 4cm (1½in) lengths with a small loop turned in the top of each (see page 29)
- Talcum powder
- 10mm (⅜in) crockery former (see page 24)
- Glue stick
- Jam jar

MIXTURES

- Carnation white
  = marble together 1 white + 2 transparent;
- Carnation green
  = 1 leaf green + 1 white

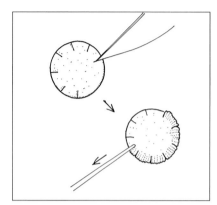

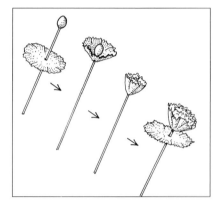

1 Form tiny balls of white around the loops on the wires and bake for 10 minutes to make the flower centres. Form a log, 6mm (¼in) thick, of the marbled white clay and cut three 1.5mm (⅟₁₆in) slices. Dust them with talc and flatten with the flat end of the former until they make paper-thin petals, about 10mm (⅜in) across. Make little cuts all round the edge and mark the edge by stroking outwards with a wool needle – this will frill the edge slightly and make it irregular.

2 Slice a petal off the board with the knife held as flat as possible. Smear a flower centre with the glue stick. Insert the end of a wire into the centre of the petal and thread it up to the ball. Gather the petal around the ball, pressing the base to secure. Repeat with the remaining two petals, gathering each loosely around the previous petal and squeezing the base.

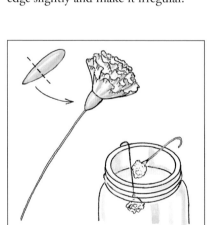

3 Form a short log of carnation green, 3mm (⅛in) thick, and point one end. Cut this end off and thread it onto the wire, pushing it up against the base of the flower. Make a hook in the end of the wire and hang the flower inside a jam jar for baking. Repeat for the remaining flowers. Bake for 10 minutes.

For instructions on how to arrange flowers in miniature vases see page 95.

FREESIAS

*The contrasting forms of these dainty flowers combine well in mixed vases,
and they can be made in many different colours.*

1 Make several stems, 1mm (½in) thick, of leaf green, each 30mm (1¼in) long, and insert a piece of beading wire (see page 84). For each spray, form three 1mm (½in) balls of light green, shape them into ovals and pat onto the tips of the stalks.

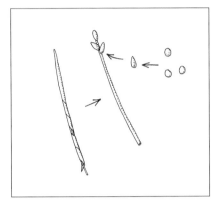

MATERIALS
- Polymer clay: transparent, blue, leaf green, yellow
- Fine beading wire

MIXTURES
- Freesia blue = 1 blue + 4 transparent;
- Light green = 4 leaf green + 1 yellow

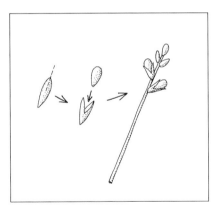

2 Form two 1.5mm (⅟₁₆in) balls of light green and two the same size of freesia blue. Shape the green balls into pointed logs and cut a slit in the end of each. Shape each blue ball into a tear drop and insert the pointed end into a green slit. Roll between your fingers lightly and press onto the stalk.

3 For the open flowers, form three 1.5mm (⅟₁₆in) tear drops of blue and insert the tip of a wool needle into each to make a trumpet. Cut across the open end to suggest petals and press the flowers onto the stalk. Carefully slice under the stalk and its flowers with your knife blade and lift onto the baking sheet. Bake for 10 minutes. To arrange the freesias, bend the stems into a gentle curve. See page 95 for tips on arranging flowers in a miniature vase.

VASES

Once you have mastered how to make a basic vase shape, you can produce a variety of vases. Try using the simulated ceramic recipes on page 23 as well as some of the suggestions for painted designs below.

MATERIALS

- Polymer clay: navy or any colour of your choice
- Paintbrush handle with a rounded end, about 5mm (³⁄₁₆in) in diameter
- Sandpaper
- Gloss varnish

1 Form a 20mm (¾in) ball of navy clay and pinch out a point in the top, rolling it between your fingers to keep it symmetrical. Trim off the point and insert the tip of a wool needle about 3mm (⅛in) into the clay. Rotate the needle in the hole to open it out and then, holding the needle at an angle, turn the vase in your fingers against the needle to flare out a lip.

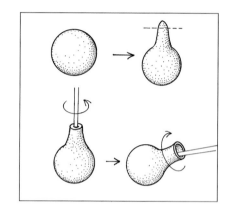

2 Insert the end of the paintbrush handle into the top of the vase and twist it gently to open it out further. Stand the vase on the board and roll the neck between your forefingers to thin it slightly and shape the vase. Pierce downwards with a wool needle to make a hole down the centre of the vase, at the same time, flattening the base. Bake for 10 minutes. Sand off any irregularities with sandpaper. Give the vase a coat of gloss varnish.

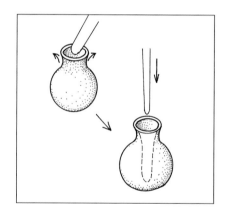

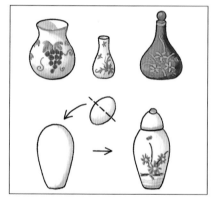

3 The illustration shows a variety of styles that can be made following these basic instructions. The lidded vases are solid shapes with a halved ball of clay pressed on top and a small ball for a handle. The bottles are simply the first stage of the vase construction with a small ball for a stopper. Try using some of the suggested painted designs to decorate your vases.

BEDSIDE LAMP

This little lamp could be adapted for any room in the house. Choose a pretty fabric with a small pattern for the lampshade and then pick out a motif to copy onto the lamp base.

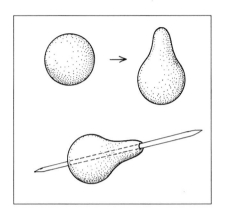

1 For the lamp base, form a 20mm (¾in) ball of white clay and pinch out one end into a point. Pierce right down through the middle with the cocktail stick and leave the cocktail stick in place. Shape into an even pear shape and press it down on the board to flatten the bottom. Bake the base for 15 minutes and remove the cocktail stick while it is still warm. Trim the top edge to make it flat and cut a groove for the wire in the bottom.

MATERIALS

- Polymer clay: white
- Cocktail stick
- Tracing paper and pencil
- Thin card
- Fine cotton fabric
- PVA glue and Superglue
- Trimmings: soutache and picot braid in toning colours to the fabric (see page 16)
- Gloss varnish
- Acrylic paint: pink, white and green.
- Fine paintbrush
- Doll's house light bulb with attached wire and plug (see page 16)

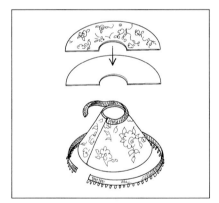

2 To make the shade, trace the shade template onto thin card and use this to cut out the fabric. Glue the fabric to the card, using PVA adhesive spread thinly and evenly. Curve the shade round and glue the edges. Glue a piece of soutache braid around the top and picot braid round the bottom. Make a shade holder as in step 6 of the Tiffany Lamp (see page 61).

3 Varnish the lamp base and then copy a motif from the fabric to paint on the base. Alternatively, you can cut out a tiny paper flower motif from a magazine and glue it on. Varnish over the paint when it is dry. Glue the shade holder to the top of the lamp and thread the wire of the bulb through the centre of the lamp so that it rests on the top of the shade holder. Attach the plug and test the lamp. Glue on the shade and, finally, glue the wire into the groove in the base so that it lies flat.

Lampshade

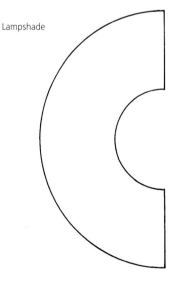

SEWING BOX

This Victorian-style work-box has simulated marquetry and a hinged lid. Inside is a collection of tiny sewing things.

MATERIALS

- Polymer clay: light brown, dark brown, ochre, beige, white, blue, green, assorted colours for the spools of thread
- Tracing paper and pencil
- Pins
- Ceramic tile
- Baking parchment
- Sandpaper
- Superglue
- Gloss varnish
- Acrylic paints: gold, silver
- Thin white card
- Beading wire (optional)

MIXTURES

- Oak wood and pine wood grains see page 27

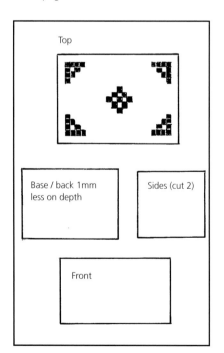

Top

Base / back 1mm less on depth

Sides (cut 2)

Front

1 Trace the box templates and cut them out. Lay the box lid template onto a block of soft clay and prick along the marquetry pattern with a pin. Roll out the oak wood grain clay on the tile until it is a little less than 3mm (⅛in) thick. Lay on the templates and cut out the pieces, leaving the waste clay in place for now. When you remove the lid template, the pricked holes should have left a faint guide.

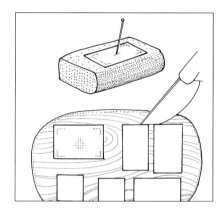

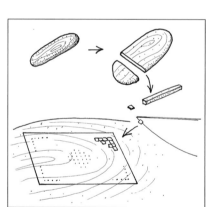

2 Form a short log, 6mm (¼in) thick, of pine wood grain clay and roll it flat until it is about 1.5mm (⅟₁₆in) thick. Cut a strip 1.5mm (⅟₁₆in) wide. Now cut tiny slices from the end of the strip and lift them on your knife onto the box lid, following the marked lines. Finally lay some baking parchment on top of the 'marquetry' and press firmly with a flat surface to press the applied pieces into the clay surface. Trim the edges again if they have distorted. Remove the waste clay from around the box pieces.

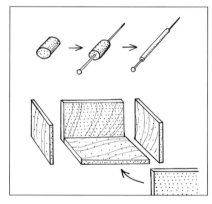

3 To make the hinge, form a log, 3mm (⅛in) thick, of dark brown clay, cut two 6mm (¼in) lengths and pierce each with a pin. Roll the logs on the board to thin them to 1.5mm (⅟₁₆in) and leave the pin in place for baking. Bake all the pieces on the tile for 30 minutes. When they are cool, remove the box parts from the tile and sand any rough edges. Assemble the box by gluing the back to the base, then the two sides and finally, the front.

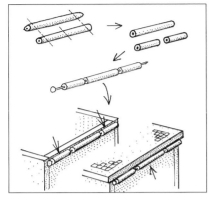

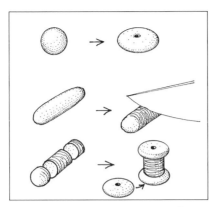

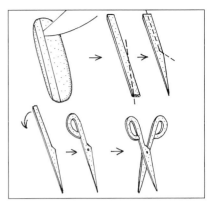

4 Cut the ends off the hinge pieces to square them and cut one in half. Assemble the hinge onto a single pin, with the longer hinge in the centre. Trim off the point of the pin and glue the outer two hinges to the top of the box back and the inner hinge to the underside rear of the lid. The lid of the box is made to overhang slightly all round. You may have to trim away a little clay to make the hinge open and shut freely. Varnish the box with gloss varnish and paint the hinge with gold paint to simulate brass.

5 To make the thread spools, form 3mm (⅛in) balls of beige clay and flatten them onto the board to make the spool ends. Pierce the centre of each with a pin. Form 3mm (⅛in) thick logs of various colours, each about 6mm (¼in) long and roll them on the board with the blade of your knife to suggest thread. Bake all the pieces for 10 minutes and then trim the coloured logs to 5mm (³⁄₁₆in) long. Glue the ends onto the coloured logs.

6 To make the scissors, roll flat some white clay on the tile until it is 1.5mm (¹⁄₁₆in) thick. Cut two strips, each 3mm (⅛in) wide and 25mm (1in) long. Make both blades identical – cut the ends to taper them and cut the tops. Curve the top end of each down and round into a handle and mark a small hole in the centre. Bake for 30 minutes then glue the two halves together. Paint with silver paint.

Instead of gluing, if you thread a snippet of beading wire through the central hole and bend over the ends, the scissors will open and shut.

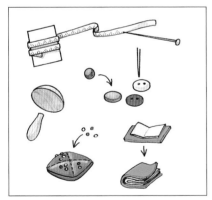

7 The remaining contents of the sewing box are made with small scraps of coloured clay. The ribbon and lace are thin strips of clay wound onto card and then baked. The darning mushroom is a dome of pine-effect clay with a handle glued on. The buttons are flattened balls with holes. See above how to make the needle book and pin cushion.

PICTURES

Picture frames can be made very successfully with polymer clays, and it is possible to simulate all sorts of different mouldings, from elaborate gilded frames to simple pine or carved mahogany and embossed silver.

MATERIALS

- Polymer clay: white
- Ceramic tile
- Metal ruler or straight edge
- Gold acrylic paint
- Graph paper
- Set square
- Picture, approximately 30 x 20mm (1¼ x ¾in)
- Tinted card
- Superglue and PVA glue
- Sharp craft knife and cutting mat or board

1 Form a log of white clay, 3mm (⅛in) thick and 20cm (8in) long, making it as even as possible. Place it on the tile and gently roll it flat until it is about 5mm (³⁄₁₆in) wide and stuck to the tile. Now push the edge of a ruler against the sides to straighten them. If there are a lot of bends and waves, lift one end, stretch it slightly and press back down onto the tile. Indent one long side with the side edge of a ruler.

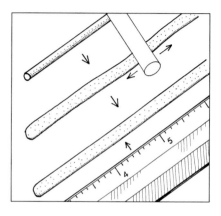

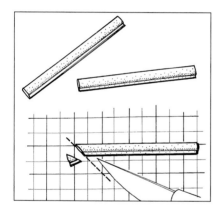

2 Bake the moulding on the tile for 20 minutes. When it is cool, paint the indented side gold, allow to dry and then remove the moulding from the tile. Cut two 45mm (1¾in) lengths and two 35mm (1⅜in) lengths from the moulding. Mitre the ends by laying each end on a piece on the graph paper and cutting at 45 degrees across a square. Be as accurate as possible and make sure that the gold side is the shorter one for each piece.

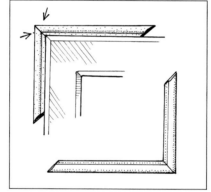

3 Squeeze a drop of Superglue onto a piece of foil and dip the end of a long side into this to coat it lightly. Using a set square to keep the pieces squared, push a short side onto the glued end. Repeat for the other pair and then glue both pairs together.

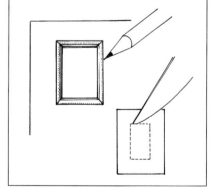

4 To make the mount, lay the frame on a piece of card and mark round it. Cut out the card just inside the line. Measure the size of your chosen picture image and draw this on the card, centred from the sides and from top to bottom. Cut this out, using a craft knife and a metal rule for neat edges.

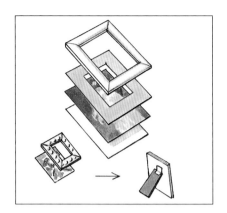

5 Glue the mount to the picture, then glue the card to the back of the frame. To make the frame sturdier, glue another piece of card to the back.

The silver photograph frames are made in the same way, using black clay and small stamps. After silvering and baking, the photographs are glued to the backs of the frames. A flap of thin clay is glued to the back with a piece of paper as a hinge to make the frame stand up.

VARIATIONS

Try using the various wood mixture clays such as pine and mahogany for frames. Stamps can be used to make more ornate gilded frames or to simulate carved wood.

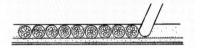

CHAPTER 8

BATHROOM MINIATURES

Polymer clay can be used to produce highly realistic miniatures for the bathroom because it simulates porcelain and plumbing so effectively. This little bathroom is based on Edwardian designs, but it can be adapted for a Victorian look by painting leaf or floral designs on the bath, wash-basin and toilet. For a more modern bathroom, mount the basin on a pedestal and place the toilet cistern at low level.

All the polymer clay miniatures in the photograph are projects in this chapter apart from: fern (page 80); bottles and jars (page 92); jug (page 89); picture (page 102).

BATH

A miniature bath made from polymer clay can look remarkably realistic because it is possible to get the clay thin enough for it to resemble enamelled cast iron. Brass taps and a plug add the finishing touches, and you could paint the outside of the bath any toning colour to match your doll's house bathroom.

MATERIALS

- Polymer clay: white, black
- A round plastic bottle with rounded shoulders; the kind often sold containing toiletries is ideal; you need one about 13cm (5in) tall and 5cm (2in) in diameter
- Plaster of Paris
- Small jug for mixing the plaster
- Sandpaper
- Matchbox covered with foil
- Gloss varnish
- Metallic powder: gold
- Beading wire
- 5cm (2in) length of gilt chain
- Superglue

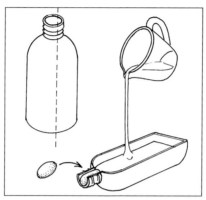

1 Cut the plastic bottle in half longitudinally, just to one side of a central line so you are left with slightly over half. (Use a serrated kitchen knife with care or scissors.) Block the top of the bottle with some scrap clay. Fill the resulting mould with water and pour this into a small jug. Sprinkle plaster onto the water until it appears above the surface and then stir. The consistency should be like that of thin cream. Allow to stand for a minute and then pour into the mould, filling it to just below the top. Leave to set overnight.

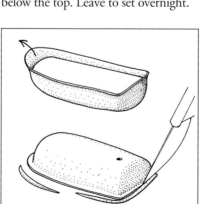

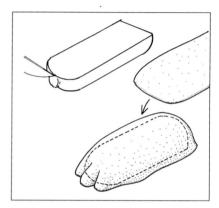

2 Remove the plaster cast from the mould and sand smooth any irregularities. Lay on the board, flat side down. Roll out approximately half a 60g (2oz) packet of white clay so that it is 3mm (⅛in) thick. Check that it is large enough to cover the plaster former, rolling it further if necessary. Lay over the former and ease the clay around the two ends, pressing it onto the former and working it down the sides so that it is about 6mm (¼in) longer than the former all round.

3 Turn the bath and former over and pull out the rounded end so that it makes a gentle curve. Place the bath and former, inverted again, on the baking sheet. Flatten the edges of the clay down all round the bath, and then trim to make an out-turned rim. Make a hole for the plug hole. Bake for 30 minutes. Leave to cool on the former and then remove carefully. Sand to remove any bumps, especially around the rim, and varnish with gloss varnish.

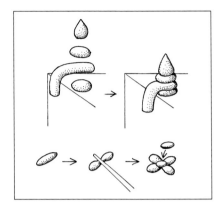

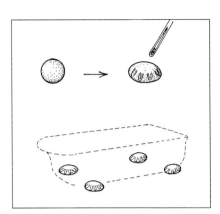

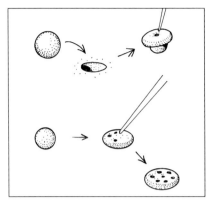

4 To make each tap, form a log, slightly less than 3mm (⅛in) thick, and cut a 13mm (½in) length. Form three 3mm (⅛in) balls, press one onto the matchbox edge, press on the end of the log, curving the other end downwards. Press another ball and, finally, a third ball, shaped into a point at the top. Make the tap tops as for the kitchen tap on page 46. Brush the tap pieces with gold powder.

5 To make the bath feet, form four 6mm (¼in) balls of clay and flatten slightly. Mark a pattern round each with the eye of a wool needle and position them on the board in two pairs. Centre the bath over them and press it down to shape the feet to the curve of the outside of the bath. Make four more 6mm (¼in) balls of clay and decorate in the same way. Brush the feet and balls with gold powder.

6 Make the plug by pressing a small ball of black clay into the hole in the bath. Pierce a hole in the centre with a pin and remove. Make the overflow by pressing flat a small ball of white clay and piercing it with a wool needle. Pierce the centre with a pin and brush with gold powder. Bake the overflow, plug, feet and tap pieces (these still on the matchbox) for 20 minutes.

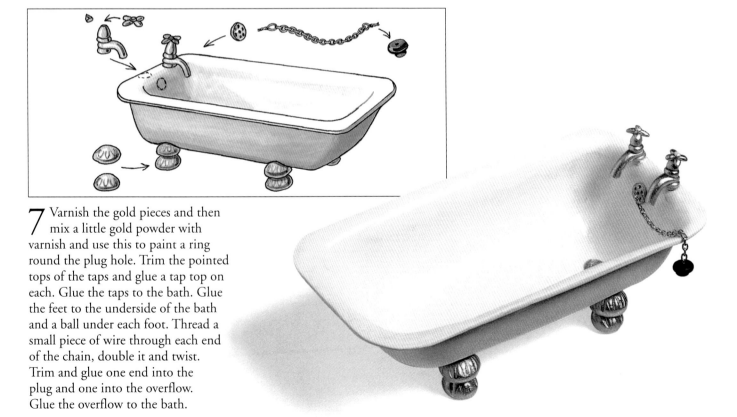

7 Varnish the gold pieces and then mix a little gold powder with varnish and use this to paint a ring round the plug hole. Trim the pointed tops of the taps and glue a tap top on each. Glue the taps to the bath. Glue the feet to the underside of the bath and a ball under each foot. Thread a small piece of wire through each end of the chain, double it and twist. Trim and glue one end into the plug and one into the overflow. Glue the overflow to the bath.

WASH-BASIN

The exposed plumbing of this little basin gives it character. For a more modern look, shape a simple pedestal of white clay and glue the basin top onto this.

MATERIALS

- Polymer clay: white, black
- Ceramic tile
- Talcum powder
- Smooth round pencil
- 20mm (¾in) marble
- Small marble
- Metallic powder: gold
- Gloss varnish
- Beading wire
- 2.5 cm (1 in) length of gilt chain
- Superglue

1 Form a 25mm (1in) ball of white clay, flatten it slightly onto the tile and smear with talcum powder to prevent sticking. Push the back up against a rounded pencil to make a splash guard. Now push the larger marble into the centre of the clay and use it to make the basin shape. Use the smaller marble to shape the inner sides more vertically. The basin should be approximately 4cm (1½in) wide and 3.5cm (1⅜in) from front to back.

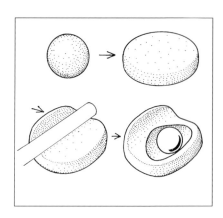

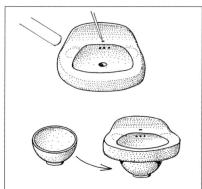

2 Roll the top lightly with the pencil to level it and indent two soap holders with the pencil end. Make three small holes for an overflow and another at the centre back for the chain attachment. Poke a plug hole in the centre. Make a large bowl, using the large marble and following the instructions on page 24. Bake the basin and the bowl for 30 minutes. When they are cool, glue the bowl underneath the basin and varnish.

3 Make taps as for the bath above but slightly smaller and glue them in place. Make a waste pipe for the basin as for the kitchen sink on page 46, and brush it with gold powder and varnish. Make a plug as for the bath on page 107. To mount, glue the basin to the wall of the bathroom and glue the drainage pipe in place underneath, trimming it to fit. If you are using the tiles (see page 112), the wash-basin is glued to the tile panel.

STOOL

*This simple 'turned wood' stool is quick and easy to make.
Try using different wood grain mixtures like pine or oak to make stools
for other rooms in the doll's house.*

1 To make the stool legs, form a log of mahogany clay 5mm (³⁄₁₆in) thick and cut three lengths, each 4cm (1½in) long. Using the darning needle, make three grooves, two close together and one further up. (See page 27 for instructions on grooving clay.) Make similar grooves on the other legs, lining up the legs to be sure that they match. Bake the legs for 20 minutes and trim the ends, again ensuring that they are all the same length.

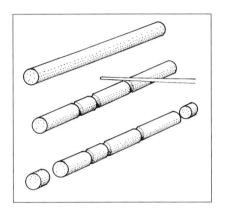

MATERIALS
- ◆ Polymer clay: dark brown, ochre, black
- ◆ Darning needle
- ◆ Superglue
- ◆ Gloss varnish
- ◆ Small piece of quilt wadding (optional)

MIXTURES
- ◆ Mahogany wood grain see page 27

2 Form a 20mm (¾in) ball of mahogany clay and flatten it onto the board until it makes a disc about 28mm (1⅛in) across. Slice off the board and place, top down, on the lined baking sheet. Push the baked legs, angled outwards slightly, into the clay to make indentations. Bake the stool top for 20 minutes. Glue the legs into their holes in the stool top. Check the stool stands level and trim the legs if necessary. Varnish with gloss varnish or polish with quilt wadding.

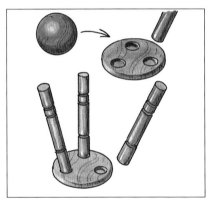

VARIATIONS

You can make a rectangular stool or plant stand using the same techniques. Cut out a rectangular top from a sheet of clay and form four grooved legs. Glue the legs vertically to the top. Form four small grooved lengths for stretchers, trim them to fit and glue between the legs.

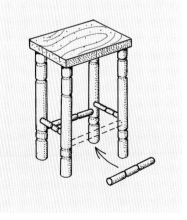

TOILET

*White porcelain, mahogany and brass are all simulated in this project
with pleasing effect. If you want to make a more modern toilet, omit the chain
and mount the cistern behind the toilet.*

MATERIALS

- Polymer clay: white, dark brown, black, ochre
- Talcum powder
- 20mm (¾in) marble
- Baking parchment and pencil
- Ceramic tile
- Sandpaper
- Superglue
- Small decorative brass hinge, 6mm (¼in) wide
- Foil
- Small matchbox or similar former, approximately 35 x 15mm (1⅜ x ⅝in), covered with foil
- Metallic powder: gold
- Gloss varnish
- 6cm (2½in) length of gilt chain
- 2 gilt S-fittings (jewellery findings) or gilt wire (see page 16)

MIXTURES

- Mahogany wood grain see page 27

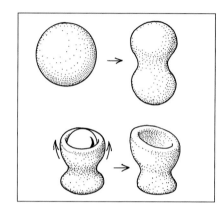

1 Form a 25mm (1in) ball of white clay and thin the middle to make an hour-glass shape. Press the bottom onto the board and dust the top with talc. Now press the marble into the centre and work the sides up around it, keeping them at least 3mm (⅛in) thick. Remove the marble and shape the bowl into an oval. The toilet should be about 3cm (1¼in) high, the same from front to back and slightly narrower.

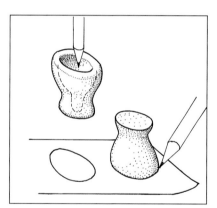

2 Push a pencil down into the centre of the bowl to make a hole and then up-end the toilet and press down onto the board to flatten the rim. Bake the toilet for 20 minutes. Varnish inside and out with gloss varnish. Now turn it upside down onto a piece of baking parchment and draw round it for a template. Repeat for a second template and place the parchment on the tile.

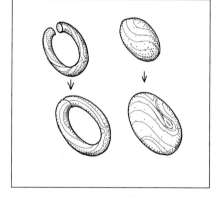

3 To make the seat, form the mahogany clay into a log 5mm (³⁄₁₆in) thick and place it over the template, curving it round into an oval, just inside the pencil line. Trim the ends and join neatly. Press the log down all round so that it is 6mm (¼in) wide and is slightly larger than the template. Form a 20mm (¾in) ball of mahogany for the lid, shape it into an oval and press down onto the second template until it slightly overlaps the pencil line.

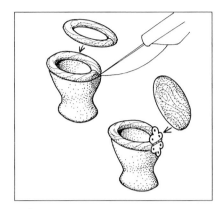

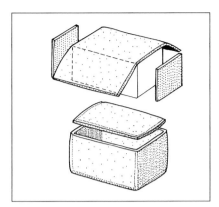

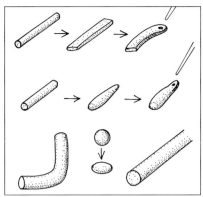

4 Bake the seat and lid on the baking parchment for 20 minutes. When cool, sand away any irregularities. Glue the seat to the top of the toilet and trim the back of both to take the hinge. Check the position for the hinge to be sure that the lid will lie flat on the seat and move freely into an upright position. Glue one end of the hinge to the inside of the lid and glue the other end to the back of the toilet and seat.

5 To make the cistern, roll out white clay 3mm (⅛in) thick and use this to cover all but one side of the foil-covered matchbox. Press a wool needle along the edges to make a decorative groove. Bake for 20 minutes and remove the former from the cistern. Cut out a lid from rolled-out clay, just larger than the cistern and using the cistern as a guide. Bake for 20 minutes and then glue to the top of the cistern.

6 Make a 10mm (⅜in) long lever of white clay with a hole in one end. Form a small tapered log, the same length, for the chain pull and make a hole in the narrow end. Form a 3mm (⅛in) thick log of white for the pipe and cut a 10cm (4in) length for the straight section and a 25mm (1in) length for the curve. Shape the latter into a right-angled bend. Flatten a 3mm (⅛in) ball into a little disc to use as a join. Brush the lever and pipes with gold powder and bake for 20 minutes.

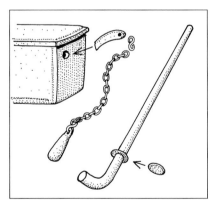

7 Varnish the cistern and pipe pieces. Make a hole in the side of the cistern with your knife tip and glue in the lever. Attach an S-fitting to each end of the chain and join these to the lever and chain pull. Trim the pipe ends to neaten them, and glue them together with the small disc between. Glue the cistern to the wall of the bathroom so that the top is about 18cm (7in) above the floor.

8 Check that the pipe is the correct length and trim if necessary. The toilet should stand in front of the pipe so that the lid rests back against it when the curved pipe is glued to the back of the toilet. If necessary, trim the curved pipe to the correct length. Glue the pipe to the under-side of the cistern. Dab glue on the base and back of the toilet and push it into place against the curved pipe.

STAMPED ART NOUVEAU TILES

Tiles are great fun to make with polymer clay. They can be stamped, painted, gilded, left matt or varnished; made in a rainbow of colours, left plain or marbled. These stylized flower tiles are typical of the Art Nouveau designs that were so popular at the end of the nineteenth century and in the early twentieth century.

MATERIALS

- Polymer clay: white
- Talcum powder
- Ceramic tile
- Tracing paper and pencil
- Pin
- Straight-bladed knife
- Graph paper
- Artist's pastel: violet, yellow, turquoise, green
- Gloss varnish
- Household filler for grouting
- Damp cloth

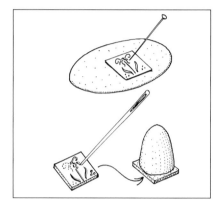

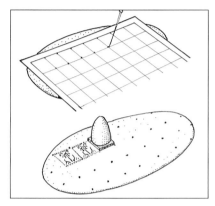

1 To make the stamp, roll out some clay on the ceramic tile to about 1.5mm (¹⁄₁₆in) thick. Trace the tile template, cut it out and lay it on the clay sheet. Prick through the paper along the main lines with a pin to transfer the outline of the design to the clay. Cut round the template and remove the surrounding clay. Remove the template and use a blunt needle to inscribe the pattern in the soft clay. Make a broad handle of scrap clay and bake both stamp and handle for 20 minutes. Glue the handle to the back of the stamp.

2 Roll out the white clay on the tile until it is of an even thickness of about 1.5mm (¹⁄₁₆in), using talcum powder as necessary to prevent it from sticking. Lay the graph paper on the clay and prick the corners of the 1cm squares to make a grid on the clay surface. (Use ½in squares if you are using inch graph paper.) Brush the surface with talc and use the stamp to impress the design onto about half of the squares. You will need about 30 tiles to tile around the wash-basin and the head of the bath.

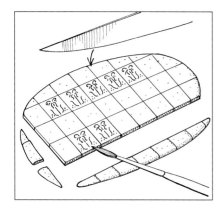

3 Rub the artist's pastels onto paper to release the powder colour and, using a fine brush, stroke the colour onto the embossed design, using the colour illustration as a guide. Use a sideways motion, which will pick out the detail. Now cut the tiles by holding the blade of a long knife along each line of pin pricks and cutting straight down. Do not attempt to move the tiles but carefully remove the incomplete squares round the edges. Bake the tiles on the ceramic tile for 30 minutes.

4 Varnish the tiles and then slice under them to remove them from the ceramic tile. You may need to cut along the lines to separate them. To make the wash-basin panel, roll out on the ceramic tile a 1.5mm (¹⁄₁₆in) thick sheet of white clay, approximately 6 x 3cm (2½ x 1¼in). Use a ruler to cut a straight top edge and arrange the little tiles in three rows onto the clay, allowing a 1mm (¹⁄₃₂in) gap between them and alternating plain and patterned tiles. Press the tiles down, trim the edges and bake on the tile for 20 minutes.

5 Mix the filler with water according to the instructions on the pack. Spoon a small quantity onto the centre of the tiled panel and use a damp cloth to work it between the tiles. Wipe away the excess, making sure that none is left on the tile surface. When the grout is completely dry, glue the panel to the wall and glue the wash-basin to it. It is possible to trim the panel with a craft knife to fit any area or around miniature plumbing and so on. Tiles around the bath are made in exactly the same way.

DELFT TILES

*These miniature tiles imitate traditional sixteenth-century Delft tiles,
and the designs shown are drawn with a dipping pen so as to create
the line effect of original Delft.*

MATERIALS

- Polymer clay: white
- Talcum powder
- Ceramic tile
- Graph paper
- Straight-bladed knife
- Gloss varnish
- Acrylic paint: blue
- Fine dipping pen (available from art shops) or a fine brush
- Household filler for grouting
- Damp cloth

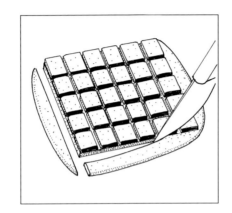

1 Follow the instructions for the Art Nouveau tiles on page 112, steps 1 to 4 (but omitting the stamps and colours) to make a panel of plain white varnished tiles of the size required. Do not grout them yet. Brush over the tiles with nail varnish remover to de-grease them.

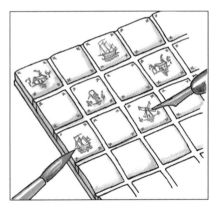

2 Mix some blue acrylic paint with an equal amount of water. Dip the pen into the paint and practise on a few spare tiles first. Make a little cross in the corner of each tile. Now draw the little motifs in the middle of alternate tiles. You can wipe mistakes off and try again. When the paint is dry, mix a pale blue wash and colour in some of the details. Leave to dry overnight, then varnish. Finally, grout the tiles as in step 5 of the Art Nouveau tiles on page 113.

OTHER BATHROOM MINIATURES

The mirror is simply a rectangular mirror framed in a mahogany wood grain frame made in the way as for the pictures on page 102.

The shelf is the single version of the shelf on page 119.

The toilet roll holder is made in the same way as the bookshelf on page 56. The roll of paper is a short log of clay, pierced with a length of cocktail stick, which is then glued into place. A piece of tissue paper is glued round the log.

The soap is simply a mixture transparent clay and a trace of colour formed into small ovals.

The back brush is made in the same way as the hairbrush on page 92, using pine marbled clay and with a longer handle.

The towel rail has two ends made like the candlestick bases on page 52. A length of cocktail stick has two small balls of clay baked on the ends and then glued to the bases.

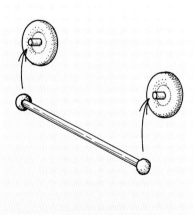

CHAPTER 9

NURSERY MINIATURES

Miniature toys have a special appeal, particularly when they have working parts. The hobby horse has turning wheels, while the little dolls have moving arms and legs. The simpler toys include a train, a teddy bear and skittles, while wall-mounted shelves and a large toy chest provide display and storage space.

Instructions for all the polymer clay miniatures in the photograph are given in this chapter apart from: lamp (page 99); clock (page 50); china (page 88); books (page 56); geranium (page 78); stool (page 109); pictures (page 102).

TOY CHEST

This is made in a similar way to the sewing box on page 100, but it has a metal hinge for strength because it is larger. The top and sides are decorated with a border of daisies, but you could glue on tiny paper motifs instead to give the effect of découpage.

MATERIALS

- Polymer clay: ochre, beige, white
- Tracing paper and pencil
- Ceramic tile
- 40mm (1½in) long miniature hinge
- Set square
- Superglue
- Matt varnish
- Fine paintbrush
- Acrylic paint: white, green, yellow

MIXTURES

- Pine wood grain see page 27

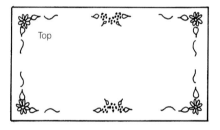

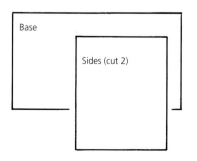

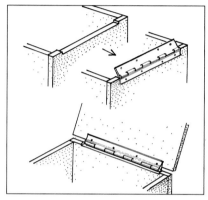

1 Trace and cut out the chest templates. Roll out the pine wood grain clay on the tile to make a sheet just over 1.5mm (¹⁄₁₆in) thick. Cut out the chest pieces, remove the waste clay and bake on the tile for 30 minutes. Remove them from the tile when they are cool. Sand any rough edges. Glue the sides to the base then glue on the front and back, using a set square to keep them vertical

Cut away the clay along the top of the back to make a slot for the hinge to sit in. Glue one side of the hinge to the outside of the top of the back and the other to the inside of the lid. Take care not to get glue into the hinge itself.

2 Varnish the box with matt varnish, allow to dry, then de-grease by brushing with nail varnish remover. Trace the outline of the daisy design onto the lid and front, and paint using a fine brush. It is easiest to paint the white daisies first, then the leaves and stems and, finally, the yellow centres. Leave overnight to dry and then varnish again with the matt varnish.

SHELVES

Shelves are quick and easy to make in polymer clay and are extremely useful in any room in the doll's house where they can be used to display all your miniature creations! Try using wood grain mixtures for mahogany, pine or oak shelves.

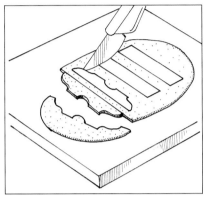

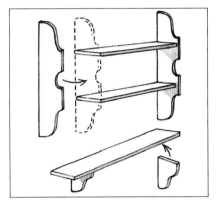

MATERIALS
- ◆ Polymer clay: white
- ◆ Tracing paper and pencil
- ◆ Ceramic tile
- ◆ Set square
- ◆ Superglue

1 Trace the templates and cut them out. Roll out the white clay on the tile until it is a little less than 3mm (⅛in) thick. Lay on the templates and cut round them. Remove the waste clay from around the pieces. Bake the pieces on the tile for 30 minutes. When they are cool, remove them from the tile and sand any rough edges.

2 Glue the shelves to one of the side pieces, using a set square to make sure that the pieces are at right angles. Glue the second side piece to the shelves. Mount the shelves by gluing them to the wall of the room. A second template is given for the single shelf used in the bathroom and above the kitchen range. For this design, mount the shelf supports under the single shelf.

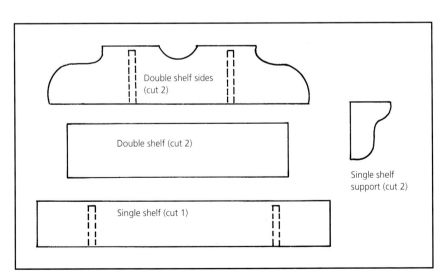

Double shelf sides (cut 2)

Double shelf (cut 2)

Single shelf (cut 1)

Single shelf support (cut 2)

DOLL

This little doll has jointed arms and legs and mohair for hair.
She is 40mm (1½in) tall or the 1:12 scale equivalent of a 46cm (18in) doll.

MATERIALS

- Polymer clay: flesh
- Pins
- Fine beading wire
- Acrylic paint: brown, blue, black, red, white
- Scrap of mohair: brown or blonde
- Fine knitting needle
- Superglue
- Fine fabric
- Fray Check (available from haberdashers)
- Scraps of lace and ribbon
- PVA glue
- Matt varnish

1 To make the head, form a ball of flesh clay, 10mm (⅜in) in diameter. Use the side of a wool needle to indent the face. Form a 1.5mm (⅟₁₆in) ball of clay and point one end for the nose. Press this onto the centre of the face, smooth the sides with a blunt wool needle and shape it into a pretty nose. Apply two thin slices from a log of flesh-coloured clay, 1.5mm (⅟₁₆in) thick, to the sides of the head for the ears. Smooth in the sides towards the face and indent them.

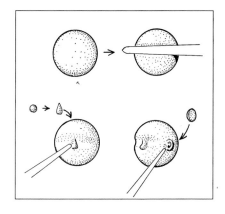

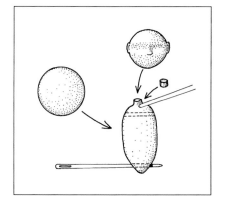

2 Form a ball, just over 10mm (⅜in) in diameter, for the body, shape it into an oval and flatten it slightly, pointing at the bottom. Push a needle through the bottom for the leg fixture and another through the shoulders. Apply a 3mm (⅛in) slice from a 3mm (⅛in) thick log to the top of the body for the neck and smooth the bottom edge in. Press the head onto the neck and smooth the join.

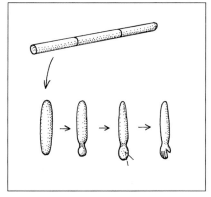

3 To make the arms, form a log 3mm (⅛in) thick and cut two 13mm (½in) lengths. Round the ends by re-rolling the logs, making them slightly longer than 13mm (½in). Make grooves about 5mm (³⁄₁₆in) from one end of each for wrists. Press the end below the wrist onto the board to flatten it and cut away a V-section with your knife to make a mitten shape. Mark fingers with the knife, slice off the board and curve round into a hand.

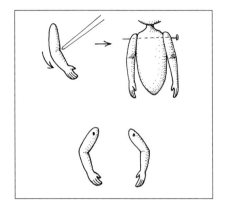

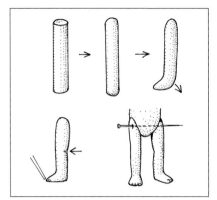

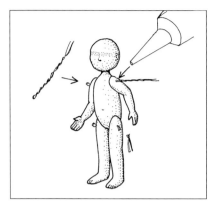

4 Mark a line with your knife for the inside of the elbow and curve the arm round. Repeat for the other arm, reversing the shaping. Press the arms lightly onto the shoulders to shape them into the correct curve and pierce right through arms and body hole with a pin. Carefully remove the arms from the shoulders for baking.

5 Cut two 20mm (¾in) lengths from a 3mm (⅛in) thick log for the legs. Re-roll to round the ends. Shape the bottom end of each into a foot by pulling the heel down and then pressing the foot flat onto the board to shape it. Mark toes and indent the legs behind the knee and heel. Press the legs lightly against the body and pierce right through legs and body hole with a pin. Carefully remove the pin and the legs, keeping the shape.

    Bake all the pieces for 15 minutes.

6 Cut two 30mm (1¼in) lengths of wire, fold each in half and twist, leaving a small loop at the fold. Push the end through the arms and body. Press the end of the wire against the second arm, keeping the wire taught and apply a drop of Superglue. Check that the arms can move freely as the glue dries. Trim the end of the wire. Repeat for the legs.

7 Brush the face with matt varnish. Draw the eyes, eyebrows and mouth outlines lightly with a pencil. You can erase any errors quite easily. Use brown acrylic paint to paint in the top eye line and fine eyebrows. Paint the irises as circles of blue (or your chosen colour), and the pupils as dots of black. Suggest a few lashes with black and paint tiny triangles of white in the eye corners. The mouth is best painted as two dots of pink or red, a darker line below and then a crescent underneath. Rub a little watery red into the cheeks. A drop of gloss varnish on the eyes adds a sparkle.

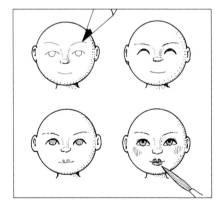

8 The hair can be curled by wrapping thin lengths around a fine metal knitting needle, securing the ends with a piece of twisted pipe cleaner and placing in a bowl of boiling water. When cool, mop dry on a towel and leave until completely dry. Cut 13mm (½in) lengths of curled hair and tease them out a little. Spread PVA glue thickly over the head and press on the hair, arranging the curls.

9 Make the knickers with two pieces of thin ribbon, gluing with PVA glue. Cut out the skirt and bodice in fine fabric and treat all the raw edges with Fray Check. Stitch the skirt into a tube, and

gather one end. Pull this onto the doll, just under the arms and draw tight. Fit the bodice and glue down, trimming to fit. Finish the dress by gluing on a thin ribbon or lace sash to cover the ends.

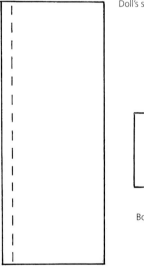

Doll's skirt

Bodice

VARIATIONS

You can make dolls in several different sizes using these basic instructions. If you would like your dolls to have shoes, do not mark toes on the feet and paint on shoes and socks after baking. Wide ribbon or lace can be used for the dresses and you can make sleeves out of tubes of ribbon or fabric.

TEDDY BEARS

Teddy bears have been a nursery favourite for nearly one hundred years.
These instructions make a little bear 25mm (1in), high but you can make them
in a range of sizes. You can texture the fur with a needle point if you wish.

1 Form a log, 3mm (⅛in) thick, of teddy bear gold and cut four 6mm (¼in) lengths. Form two of these into ovals for the legs and thin one end of each. Press the other end down lightly onto the board to flatten it for the foot. Flatten two tiny balls of ochre and press one onto the bottom of each foot for pads. Place the two legs, side by side and splayed out.

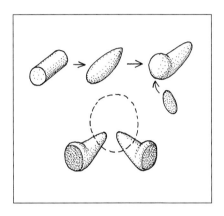

MATERIALS
- ◆ Polymer clay: yellow, ochre, white, black
- ◆ Scrap of narrow ribbon

MIXTURES
- ◆ Teddy bear gold
  = 3 ochre + 1 yellow + trace of white

2 Form a 10mm (⅜in) ball of gold clay for the body. Shape it into an oval and press onto the legs. Shape the other two 6mm (¼in) lengths into arms and apply oval patches of ochre for the pads. Press the arms onto the top of the body, curving them round. Form an 8mm (⅜in) ball of gold, pinch out a small snout and press gently onto the top of the body for the head.

3 Flatten two 1.5mm (¹⁄₁₆in) balls of gold onto the board for the ears, slice off the board and apply, edge-on to the top of the head, using the wool needle to make ear holes and press them on. Poke eye sockets with the needle and fill each with a tiny ball of black. Pat a thin slice of black onto the snout for the nose. Bake for 10 minutes.

Tie a ribbon round the teddy's neck in a bow.

HOBBY HORSE

*A dappled grey hobby horse with bright red reins and turning wheels
is a delightful traditional toy. You can use black embroidery silk instead
of mohair for the mane.*

MATERIALS

- Polymer clay: white, red, black, ochre, beige
- Cocktail stick
- 6mm (¼in) former (see page 24)
- 2 pins
- Artist's pastel: grey
- Acrylic paint: white
- Black mohair or embroidery silk
- Superglue
- PVA glue

MIXTURES

- Pine wood grain (see page 27)

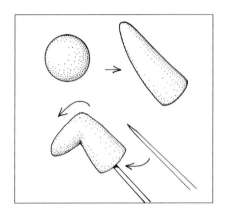

1 To make the horse's head, form a 15mm (⅝in) ball of white clay. Shape it into a 40mm (1½in) long cone with a blunt point. Bend the pointed end downwards for the horse's head. Insert the point of a cocktail stick into the base of the neck and trim so that 40mm (1½in) protrudes to make the hobby horse pole. Brush the head with a light dusting of grey pastel, leaving the clay lighter on the nose and chest.

2 Form a log, 1mm (¹⁄₃₂in) thick, of red clay and roll flat into a long strip, about 1.5mm (¹⁄₁₆in) wide. Cut lengths from this and wrap them round the head to make a bridle. Make two small cones of white clay for ears and press them onto the top of the head, indenting ear holes with a wool needle. Brush grey pastel onto the ears.

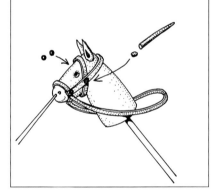

3 Poke two holes for eye sockets and fill them with small balls of black. Make holes for the nostrils and a line for a mouth. Roll out a strip of red clay as for the bridle and apply loosely in a loop from the bridle round the back of the neck for the reins. Press on small slices of black log for studs on the bridle.

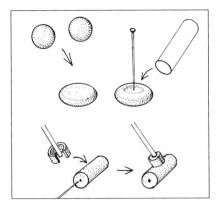

4 Form two 6mm (¼in) balls of red clay and flatten onto the board to make two 10mm (⅜in) discs. Indent the centre of each with the former and make a tiny hole in the centre with a pin. Form a 5mm (³⁄₁₆in) thick log of pine clay and cut a 15mm (⅝in) length for the axle. Make a deep hole in each end with a pin. Wrap a small strip of pine clay around the trimmed end of the cocktail stick and press it onto the centre of the axle.

5 Bake the horse, axle and wheels for 20 minutes. Paint dapples with white paint over the head and neck. Glue a fringe of mohair to the horse's neck for a mane, tucking it behind the reins. Pierce a pin through each wheel, trim the end and glue into the ends of the axle, leaving enough space for the wheels to turn freely. Glue the cocktail stick to the head and into the hole in the axle.

OTHER TOYS

The little train in the photograph is made by cutting square shapes from unkneaded clay blocks. Jewellery peg and loop findings are used for the couplings.

The skipping rope is simply a piece of cord attached to handles shaped from pine clay and the skittles are grooved pine clay with a mahogany wood grain ball. The bucket in the photograph on page 118 is a potted vessel with a painted scene on the sides and a wire handle added.

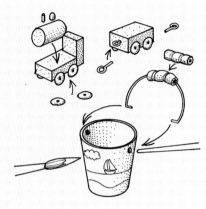

FURTHER READING AND SUPPLIERS

If you are making and decorating a doll's house, you may find the following books useful.

DODGE, Venus, *Dolls' House Needlecrafts*, David & Charles, Newton Abbot, 1995

EATON, Faith, *The Ultimate Doll's House Book*, Dorling Kindersley, London, 1994

HEASER, Sue, *Making Miniature Dolls with Polymer Clay*, Ward Lock, London, 1999

LODDER, Carol and Nigel, *Making Dolls' House Interiors*, David & Charles, Newton Abbot, 1994

Doll's house magazines are an excellent source of inspiration and projects. They also contains many advertisements for mail order suppliers of miniature materials such as those used in the projects in this book.

AUSTRALIA
The Australian Miniaturist Magazine
PO Box 467
Carlingford
NSW 2118

UNITED KINGDOM
Dolls House and Miniature Scene
EMF Publishing
EMF House 5–7 Elm Park
Ferring
West Sussex BN12 5RN

Dolls House World
Avalon Court
Star Road
Partridge Green
West Sussex RH13 8RY

UNITED STATES
Dollhouse Miniatures
Kalmbach Publishing Co.
PO Box 1612
Waukesha
WI 53187

Polymer Clay Organisations
(Please send a SAE when enquiring about membership)

UNITED KINGDOM
The British Polymer Clay Guild
Meadow Rise
Wortham, Diss
Norfolk IP22 1SQ

UNITED STATES
The National Polymer Clay Guild
Suite 115-345
1350 Beverly Road
McLean, VA 22101

Polymer Clay Suppliers
Polymer clays are available in craft and art material shops and also by mail order from craft, jewellery and doll's house suppliers. If you have problems finding the clays, the following suppliers should be able to help.

AUSTRALIA
C.A.M.
197 Blackburn Road
Syndal
VIC 3149
(Modelene)

Staedtler (Pacific) Pty. Ltd
PO Box 576
1 Inman Road
Dee Why, NSW 2099
(Fimo)

CANADA
KJP Crafts
PO Box 5009 Merival Depot
Nepean
ONT K2C 3H3
(Sculpey III, Premo)

Staedtler Mars Ltd
6 Mars Road, Etobicoke
Ontario M9V 2K1
(Fimo)

NEW ZEALAND
Golding Handcrafts
PO Box 9022
Wellington
(Du-Kit, Fimo)

Zigzag Polymer Clay Supplies
8 Cherry Place
Casebrook
Christchurch
(Premo, Sculpey III)

UNITED KINGDOM
CATS Group
PO Box 12
Saxmundham
Suffolk IP17 3PB
(Cernit)

Edding (UK) Ltd
Merlin Centre, Acrewood Way
St Albans
Hertfordshire AL4 0JY
(Sculpey III, Premo)

Kars & Co, B.V.
PO Box 272
Aylesbury, Bucks
HP18 9YX
(Creall-Therm)

Specialist Crafts
PO Box 247
Leicester LE1 9QS
(will export Formello worldwide)

Staedtler (UK) Ltd
Pontyclun
Mid Glamorgan
CF72 8YJ
(Fimo)

UNITED STATES
American Art Clay Co Inc
4717 W. Sixteenth Street
Indianapolis, 46222-2598
(Fimo)

Clay Factory of Escondido
PO Box 460598
Escondido
CA 92046-0598
(Cernit, Sculpey III, Premo)

Current information on suppliers can be found on the World Wide Web site:
http://www.heaser.demon.co.uk

INDEX